Forgotten Faces
A Window Into Our Immigrant Past

Written and Photographed
by Ronald William Horne

Introduction, History and Culture Chapters
by Lisa Montanarelli

Edited by Geoffrey Link

Personal Genesis Publishing
San Francisco, California

Forgotten Faces – A Window Into Our Immigrant Past
© 2004 by Ronald William Horne

Manufactured in the United States of America.

Published by Personal Genesis Publishing, 110 Pacific Ave., #204, San Francisco, CA 94111

First Edition. Black and White Edition with Color Plates

ISBN 0-9747395-2-9 8.5" X 11" Black and White with Color Plates

1. Photography – History – 20th Century
2. Photography – Portrait

Cover Design: Ron Horne
Photography: Ron Horne
Photo Editing and Layout: Ron Horne
All text unless otherwise noted: Ron Horne
Introduction, History and Culture Chapters: Lisa Montanarelli
Captions: well-written captions: Lisa Montanarelli, all others: Ron Horne
Editing (except captions): Geoff Link

Acknowledgments

We wish to thank:

Katherine Atkinson, Director of Cemeteries, San Francisco Archdiocese for her vision and understanding, and **Jim Cornett** and the rest of the Holy Cross's wonderful staff for their commitment and assistance researching archival information

Holy Cross Cemetery and the San Francisco Archdiocese for their generous permission and support

Sebastian Fechera, Manager and **Giuseppe Timpano**, Facility Manger of **the Italian Cemetery** for their kind support and considerate permission, and **Andrew Canepa,** Assistant Manager for his eye for detail, considerable depth of knowledge and always astute historical insights

Jay Ruby for his important commentary on postmortem photographs and his invaluable contributions to the understanding and appreciation of the art

Laurel Gabel for her informed feedback, extremely helpful input and wonderful attitude, which made a tangible, discernable and valuable difference towards the improved quality of this work

Fran Link and Trina Lopez of The California Historical Society for their patient assistance and constructive research guidance

Mark Fontana of Fontana Monuments for his many years of industry experience and guidance, **Richard Stannard** of J.A. Dedouch company for his insights and valued history on the manufacture of memorial portraits

David Hopper and Michael Sandquist of Paradise Pictures for their generous time reviewing the technology chapter and their considerable expertise on all aspects of memorial portraits

The Association of Gravestone Studies for their wealth of resources, extremely helpful and knowledgeable members and ongoing enthusiasm for the project

Dr. Stanley B. Burns and J.R. Olivero for their outstanding archives, considerable contributions to the art and support of the project

Matt Hucke for his time, excellent website and obvious depth of knowledge

Helen Sclair for her unbridled enthusiasm, informed commentary and limitless dedication to the increased awareness of the cemetery industry and its issues

Dejan for his translations and thoroughly courteous interactions

Robert Carminati whose 40 plus years as an industry artisan provided valuable guidance

Patti Verbanas and Joel Grover of *Art and Antiques* magazine for their insight and risk taking where others preferred to remain cautious or indifferent

and most certainly, the **unnamed portrait photographers** who took the original photographs capturing the character in these vibrant faces **and the artisans** who fired them on enamel , preserving these images for us to see and enjoy after decades of anonymity.

- Special Acknowledgments -

Lisa Montanarelli

From the day Lisa agreed to edit a proposal I had written for *Forgotten Faces*, she was an enthusiastic and tireless advocate for its publication. She wrote its first article, discovered fascinating stories in newspaper archives and produced important chapters on its history and culture. I am indebted to Lisa for her important contributions and outstanding skills that not only helped make the book much better but served as a key ingredient in making it happen at all.

Geoff Link

Geoff saw the pictures of the portraits when they were just a bundle of photos. He told me what needed to be done to make them a unified whole that made a statement. At every step, he guided me towards making this project as professional as possible. Then he did the nicest thing anyone has ever done for me – he volunteered to edit the book and make my writing readable. He is a very busy man with little spare time. Without his generous assistance, you would not be reading this book at all, or if you did, you'd likely be frowning at every struggling sentence. Geoff made the story a book and the book a story.

Gary Collison

From the day Gary reviewed the first photographs of the portraits – before almost anyone else - he was extremely supportive, encouraging and generous in his praise. I am indebted to him for giving me the early impetus to keep this project going forward. Coming from someone with his breadth of expertise, his helpful commentary made the difference that made the difference.

Deborah Horne

Deborah, my wife of thirty years, shared in every picture and cherished every word. She never lacked for praise and encouragement. She never doubted. She never wavered. She provided patience without limit and love between the lines. Who could ask for more?

Clyde B. Horne

My father wondered how and why I would leave a lucrative, two-decade career in the tech industry to write a book about dead people. I often wondered along with him. But his support was constant, his trust unremitting and his pride without question. He has been that way all my life. Without that foundation, none of these words would have found the light of day.

Photographic Contributors

I am genuinely thankful for the generous contributions of the following photographers and industry experts. Their photographs present examples of photo-ceramic memorial portraits from across the United States and Europe and greatly expand our appreciation of this funerary art form.

Richard E. Meyer is Professor Emeritus of English and Folklore at Western Oregon University, Monmouth, Oregon. He has edited the books *Cemeteries and Gravemarkers: Voices of American Culture* and *Ethnicity and the American Cemetery*, is co-author (with art historian Peggy McDowell) of *The Revival Styles in American Memorial Art,* and for eleven years served as editor of *Markers: Annual Journal of the Association for Gravestone Studies.* His published work in literature includes studies of the British poet George Crabbe, several articles on American outlaw ballads and legends and, in the area of material necrology, scholarly articles on contemporary logger gravemarkers in the Pacific Northwest, trail imagery on Oregon pioneer gravemarkers, San Francisco's Presidio Pet Cemetery, the forms and uses of humour in the graveyard, and World War I Western Front battlefield cemeteries.

Professor Meyer has presented more than seventy professional papers at meetings of scholarly organizations and has published in excess of fifty book reviews in various scholarly journals. From 1986-1996 he chaired the Cemeteries and Gravemarkers section of the American Culture Association, and in 1998 was recipient of the Association for Gravestone Studies' Harriete M. Forbes Award for excellence in gravestone studies. He has served as President of the Oregon Folklore Society and has conducted fieldwork in cemeteries throughout the U.S. and Europe, and has photographed in excess of 20,000 grave monuments. His major work in progress is a projected book on America's Tomb of the Unknown Soldier in Arlington National Cemetery.   *Email Contact: MeyerR@wou.edu*

Cathy Ward has a Masters degree in ceramics from the Royal College of Art, London. In the 1980's she visited the monumental *Isola di San Michele* Venice, and started documenting the graves. Since then, she has photographed cemeteries in Europe, America and Canada. Other projects include photographing depressed seaside amusements and austerely crafted food wagons (www.Wagontrain.org); recording forgotten museums, and much that is overlooked or destined to disappear. Interests: embrace folk traditions and popular culture in both sculpture and installation. Created "Transromantik"with Eric Wright for the Chamber of Pop Culture, The Horse Hospital, London, is an associate member of the Royal British Society of Sculptors and contributes to the Strange Attractor Journal.
Web URL Contact: www.cward.info

Constance Clare has photographed funerary art throughout Europe and provided the Italian monument photo on page 93. She is certified by the American Society for the Alexander Technique has a private practice in the San Francisco Bay Area. She also teaches at ACT in San Francisco.   *Email contact - constance_clare@yahoo.com*

Dedication

Carmela "Connie" Horne
January 9, 1920 to July 5, 1998

To my mother who was not allowed, by cemetery and church policy, to have a memorial portrait on her head-stone. This book and this page are dedicated to her memory, her love and her spirit.

Table of Contents

The silhouette of the Glover Angel at dusk provides an element of reverence as the night descends upon Holy Cross Cemetery.

Foreword

It has always been about the faces in the photographs. The first time I glanced down to notice the portrait of Louise Bajada on her tombstone – it stopped me in my tracks. It was a striking image. Its soft, gilt-edged sepia tones made it distinctive and appealing. It stood apart from the many, full-colored, modern portraits that populate the spacious of grounds of Holy Cross Cemetery.

Then I noticed the date —1928— more than 75 years ago. Amazing. How could such a work of art be outdoors for all that time and remain in such excellent condition? Louise's old photograph and that instant of surprise served as the genesis for *Forgotten Faces*. From that point on, the people in the portraits had a life of their own.

When I looked closely at Louise's gravestone portrait, I felt a palpable chill and conflicting emotions. I observed the youthful face of the child buried beneath my feet. I seemed connected to this person as if I knew her, though separated by an unbreachable chasm in time. It was disorienting. This is the curious power of these portraits. They are a bewildering blend of life and death. They stir the heart, then play tricks with the mind. They remain different from normal photographs. Memorial portraits place you on the boundary of time but you are not sure which side you are standing on.

My first impulse was to find a book about these fascinating time capsules. I wanted to know how they were made, their history and see portraits from other cemeteries. But I found no book, no explanation of the technology and very few people who knew much about these ceramic photographs found only in the fields of our dead.

I began showing the photographs to friends and colleagues. I was impressed with their reactions. Everyone seemed to engage with these faces from the past and many people got surprisingly emotional about these pictures, some nearly a century old.

I began to survey the 284 acres of Holy Cross Cemetery for these ceramic secrets from our past. Occasionally, they came in clusters. I photographed each one. It was fun. I relished taking the photos home and exploring them. San Francisco's history seemed to come alive in these faces. Stories emerged. The epitaphs provided context for the images. Vital young men and women perished in their prime, women died during childbirth, men in the line of duty and spouses shortly after the death of their loved ones.

Young girls still cradled their dolls, twirled lace parasols and dressed in white from head to toe excited about their first Holy Communion. Boys proudly wore suits, pleased to look older than they really were. Mothers and daughters, mothers and sons, entire families—their lives seemed to open up before me. I kept taking photographs of these personal treasures. It was like finding Rembrandts in the attic.

After documenting hundreds of portraits, an idea for a collection of photographs began to grow. Encouraged by others, I sketched out a proposal for a book. Determining that I needed a professional editor to tell the story well, I was referred to Lisa Montanarelli to edit my first book proposal. She is the co-author of the fast-selling *The First Year– Hepatitis C: An Essential Guide for the Newly Diagnosed* and came highly recommended as a free-lance editor.

Like many who saw the faces in the photographs, Lisa took a personal interest in them. She asked if she could write an article about the portraits. She queried Patti Verbanas, the managing editor of *Art and Antiques* magazine, who responded enthusiastically by making room for a short piece and an appealing portrait of young Mina Maffei, who died in 1921. With guidance and help from members of the Association for Gravestone Studies, the California Historical Society and the generous support of Katherine Atkinson, director of Catholic Cemeteries in San Francisco, the book, like the pictures, began to develop its own momentum.

Lisa, a superb researcher with a doctorate in literature from University of California at Berkeley, unearthed fascinating, 80-year-old newspaper headlines on several portrait subjects from archives of the San Francisco Chronicle and the Examiner. The portraits kept surprising everyone who investigated them. Lisa asked if she could write the book's introduction and a history of the portraits. The people in the portraits, quiet for so long, seemed determined to tell their story.

I never intended to write a book. I simply felt that Louise's portrait and the others I discovered all around her were remarkably beautiful. I was impressed at their age and superb condition. I was surprised that they had been lost to the pages of history and art. It seemed impossible that this beautifully preserved art, hidden in plain sight for nearly a century, had never been comprehensively explored.

Literary professionals also found the story of this oversight deserving of attention. An old friend of three decades, Geoff Link, generously volunteered to edit the work of this first-time author. Geoff, who has had two full-time jobs, as daily newspaper copyeditor and director of a nonprofit, for as long as I have known him, somehow found the time to smooth my tangled text into readable, coherent sentences. These faces from the past would be seen in the present again.

My motives now are simple. I believe these portraits represent remarkable works of art. I consider them compelling and valuable supplements to our history. They show us unheralded immigrants trying to forge new lives — not cultural icons or embellished historical legends. There is value in that. These surviving photographs of our ancestors deserve recognition, preservation and protection. The portraits, through the eyes of their subjects, compel us to do so.

I urge amateur and professional photographers throughout the United States to explore their cemeteries and capture the essence of these forgotten faces. I appeal to historians to help recover this hidden heritage. I encourage gravestone enthusiasts, who are the real experts and true guardians of the art, to document them and organize their findings. To all those who find these portraits in their own backyards as captivating, document these treasures for future generations, for history, for the importance and the fun of it.

Chicago, Atlanta, New York and many other major cities unknowingly harbor these photo-ceramic portraits in the sleepy calm of their burial grounds. Yet, more people vandalize these relics than preserve them. I hope *Forgotten Faces* helps to reverse that ratio by serving as the catalyst for preserving these unique art works, while it is still possible to do so.

If you experience the faces of these portraits as so many do—reaching across the partition of time and coming alive in the mind's eye—then this book will fulfill its objective, to acknowledge these portals to the past as valued art and artifacts. Louise Bajada and all the faces in the portraits would concur. It is the desire in their eyes, still evident for all to see, that made it happen.

Ron Horne, 2004

INTRODUCTION

By Lisa Montanarelli

In *Essays upon Epitaphs I*, William Wordsworth describes the ancient Greek and Roman custom of burying their dead by the roadside. The gravestone often featured the inscription *Sta Viator* or "Pause, Traveler," inviting passers-by to think of "life as a journey—death as a sleep overcoming the tired wayfarer." As Wordsworth writes, "Pause, Traveler" also gives "a voice" to the "language of the senseless stone" (54). Through personification, the tombstone speaks, acquiring qualities of a living person, in this case a voice, while the traveler pauses—or stops dead—trading places with the senseless stone.

Unlike the ancient roadside tombs, monuments displaying photographs are often hidden from sight. Yet they have an even stronger effect of bringing the dead to life and halting us in our tracks. A face peering out from a gravestone calls attention to the person whose life the stone memorializes. It invites curiosity about who that person was and how she lived and died.

When I first saw Ron Horne's digital images of these portraits, I—like so many others who have seen them—wanted to get to know the people portrayed. In a sense, we can know them by reading between the lines of their epitaphs and researching their lives in local newspapers and cemetery archives. The *San Francisco Chronicle* and *Examiner* tell the stories of San Francisco Police Officer Benjamin G. Root, killed in a motorcycle accident, Bridie Kearny, mysteriously shot at a wedding, and Private James Kendrick, who survived eight charges in World War I only to die in a café brawl (*p. 34*).

In another sense, we cannot know the people shown in these portraits. They are dead, as are the mourners who chose their photographs and stones. They are no more possible to know than characters in a book. A tombstone is a personal observation of grief as well as a public memorial. The newspaper tells us about people's public lives, but many more private stories remain untold. Benjamin Root's wife Helen remarried, but was buried with her first husband 60 years after his death. The epitaph on the stone—"To one who I dearly love"—says a lot, but also very little. The saying that they took their secrets to the tomb holds true.

Since 1999, Horne has photographed more than 500 portraits mounted on tombstones in Holy Cross Cemetery. These images, dating from 1899 to 1947, represent immigrants from at least 28 nations, including Mexico, Jamaica, Russia, China, the Philippines, and many countries in Latin America, Europe, and the British Isles.

Each portrait in *Forgotten Faces* is a photographic image fired on an enamel or porcelain tablet. In 1854 two French inventors patented a method of fixing a photographic image on enamel or porcelain by firing it in a kiln. More durable than the daguerreotype, these ceramic photographs were used for home viewing well into the 20th century, when the more convenient paper photos replaced them. Ninety-nine percent of enamel photos manufactured today are mounted on gravestones (Carpenter).

These photographs go by a variety of names. Ron Horne follows contemporary manufacturers in calling them "memorial portraits." Photographer John Yang notes that these they were called "enamels" in the early 20th century (xix). Photo historian Jay Ruby refers to the monuments as "photographic tombstones" (147ff), and Joseph J. Inguanti describes the photo-ceramic *rittratti* (or "portraits") that early 20th-century Italian immigrants displayed on grave markers and on the walls of their homes (16).

Though the custom of attaching ceramic photographs to tombstones is still practiced today, there is scarcely any literature on the subject. The existing literature, which I review in Chapter Two, includes a handful of scholarly essays, some ads from 19th-century magazines and newspapers, and John Yang's *Mount Zion Sepulchral Portraits*, the first and only other photo book on these haunting images. As recent writing on this topic has been largely academic, *Forgotten Faces* is in a sense the first book written for a popular audience as well as a scholarly one.

One of the chief purposes of *Forgotten Faces* is to raise public awareness of the portraits and their need for preservation. It is hard to determine the number of photographic tombstones in the United States. Many of these monuments hide in remote parts of cemeteries and have never been documented. In *Silent Cities*, Kenneth Jackson and Camilo José Vergara estimate hundreds of thousands, but this includes contemporary graves and those from the last half of the 20th century (47). Based on consultations with experts from around the country, Horne estimates that 25,000 to 35,000 have survived from the early 20th century. He warns of their ongoing disappearance due to exposure and vandalism. We hope *Forgotten Faces* will inspire you to protect this vanishing folk art.

Works Cited

Carpenter, Woodrow. Enamel Photography. Society of Dutch Enamellers. http://www.enamellers.nl/english/carpenter1.htm

Inguanti, Joseph J. 2000. Domesticating the Grave: Italian-American Memorial Practices at New York's Calvary Cemetery. In *Markers XVII*. Edited by Richard E. Meyer. Greenfield, Massachusetts: Association for Gravestone Studies.

Jackson, Kenneth and Camilo José Vergara. 1989. *Silent Cities*. New York: Princeton Architectural Press.

Ruby, Jay. 1995. *Secure the Shadow: Death and Photography in America*. Cambridge and London: MIT Press.

Wordsworth, William. 1974. Essays on Epitaphs I. In *The Prose Works of William Wordsworth*. Vol. 2. Edited by W.J.B. Owen and Jane Worthington Smyser. London: Oxford University Press, 45-119.

Yang, John. *Mount Zion Sepulchral Portraits*. 2001. New York: D.A.P/Distributed Art Publishers, Inc.

CHAPTER ONE

The Discovery: Hidden in Plain Sight

Every day and night since 1928, Louise Bajada's open eyes have gazed across the rolling fields of the Colma Valley with silent intensity. Her ageless expression reveals a composure beyond a girl of 11. Stand before her portrait seven decades later and she still seizes the moment and makes herself real.

That Louise passed away 76 years ago does not diminish the character in her youthful face. Why did she die so young? Did her mother, Carmela, buried with her, have other children? Where is her father? The story is untold as we try to read between the lines. This is the legacy of Louise's portrait. Her photograph, as fresh as the day it was taken, compels us to know more about this face - this life cut short some seven decades ago.

The Present Meets the Past – Face to Face

Louise's unyielding gaze still holds our attention. Through the photographer's eternal lens, we bond with the vibrant spirit of her determined expression. In this moment, we come face to face with the past.

And so it is with the hundreds of others who also come alive across the gulf of time through the photographic portraits and revealing epitaphs of Holy Cross Cemetery in Colma, California. The largest and oldest cemetery in this "City of Cemeteries," Holy Cross presents a rich tapestry of California's past in the early, tumultuous decades of the 20th century.

Just south of San Francisco, the Montara range and its sister peak, San Bruno Mountain, defines a five-mile valley connecting the Pacific Ocean with San Francisco Bay. Nestled in this geological channel lies Colma; with an active population of 1,200 and nearly a million deceased residents, this valley is best known for the pioneers and historical figures from California's Wild West now buried here.

The celebrated names of Wyatt Earp, Levi Strauss, Adolph Sutro, A.P. Gianini, Claus Spreckels, James Flood, Thomas Larkin, Charles deYoung and William Randolph Hearst dominate the valley's gentle floor. From 1902 to 1942, San Francisco moved its own cemeteries outside its city limits, transferring 90,000 interments to this quiet community.

Imposing mausoleums in the classic style of ancient Greece and Rome define the tombs of these rich and famous. Among these great temples resides a small army of marble angels, arms pointing skyward and heads bent in mourning; these angels of stone grant timeless testimony to the wealthy, renowned and accomplished from California's storied past. But another history, maybe more meaningful to us today, is also embodied here.

In 1999, I hiked this Colma landscape with my camera, photographing architectural and angelic archetypes. One day I happened to glance down to notice a small but skillfully executed portrait of a young girl affixed to a half-buried stone. The cemeteries of Colma contain thousands of headstones that feature ceramic photographs of the deceased. But this

Louise J. Bajada
1917 — 1928   Age 11 years, 2 months

The first portrait to capture the author's attention. It served as the genesis for *Forgotten Faces*. See Louise's color portrait - Page I.

Louise's portrait once included another person. Can you find the clues? During this era many families did not possess photographs of their children alone. They selected a group portrait and the artisan who fired the photograph would crop to isolate the subject. Did you locate the visible thumb and painted-over fingers of someone else's hand on Louise's right shoulder? You may have noticed the polka-dot remnants of clothing on the right side of the picture as well.

one's distinctive style and apparent age caught my eye. In muted colors, the oval picture of an 11-year-old child, Louise Bajada, stood just inches above the ground. Her epitaph revealed 75 winters' wear, but her image was pristine. Through some obscure technology, the subtle smile of this young child has remained intact for seven decades.

The photograph represented an appealing example of portraiture art. The child's eyes stared upward and directly into my camera, deliberately engaging any viewer. That instant in time, three quarters of a century ago, linked Louise with me in the present. Moved by the child's charm and amazed by the unspoiled portrait despite its obvious age, I photographed it in macro and returned to documenting the architecture and archetypes.

Then, a few steps away, I found another portrait from the same era, also in excellent condition. In sepia tones, the picture revealed a young man of 21 who passed away in 1927. His epitaph disclosed a captivating name, Defendente Guerra, "Defender of War." His open collar, woolen jacket and calm demeanor seemed to belie the weight of his name. Defendente's (p. 46) expression speaks as clearly today as it did seven decades ago. His picture's perfect condition provoked a question: What technology existed in the early 1900s that could preserve photographs so well despite outdoor exposure for years. Impressed by the pictorial quality and intriguing name, I photographed Defendente's picture, as well.

Even as I set up my camera, I noticed another nearby portrait that proved to be equally intriguing: a woman of 25 with a broad smile and perfectly coiffed waves of flowing hair. However, this 74-year-old photograph seemed out of place on a gravestone. Edna Wolters (p. 37), who died in 1928, covered herself with a large and discreetly positioned ostrich feather. Was she an entertainer, a dancer, an actress? Wolters' portrait presented a memoriam with amusement, mystery and a need to know more.

Struck by the age, condition and workmanship of the portraits, I marked this spot on the map of the sprawling cemetery, planning to return and investigate these surprising portraits at a later date.

Hidden in Plain Sight

Initially, I assumed their presence was common knowledge. They were too unusual to go unnoticed. To find out more, I searched for books on the subject. I found none. Surprised, I began to pursue my investigation with more dedication. I contacted the California Historical Society, the Association for Gravestone Studies and the National Tombstone Transcription Project, requesting publications on the subject. They had no books on old gravestone portraits. Information on monuments, epitaphs and famous burials abounded. But nothing dedicated or definitive existed on memorial portraits from this time period.

Some esoteric articles mentioning photo-ceramic portraits were eventually discovered. Although interesting and perceptive, none of these articles or book chapters provided in-depth insights on the technology, the history or the prevalence of these near century-old photo-artifacts.

Utilizing the term "sepulcher monuments," an Internet search finally yielded a book by John Yang entitled *Mt. Zion Sepulchral Portraits*. Yang, an accomplished architect and photographer, had documented New York's Mt. Zion Jewish Cemetery where portraits from the same era were found in abundance. Well photographed, the pictures were displayed in an exhibit at John Stevenson's Gallery in New York.

Approximately 35 portraits, greatly enlarged, were displayed at the gallery and in the book. The majority of the enamels, as he accurately calls them, presented severely decayed and eroded subjects. Many of the faces were completely or partially unrecognizable. Yang explored the degeneration of the portraits as an art form in and of itself. In this state of advanced decay they became a form of gothic art revealing ghostly shadows of their original subjects. Yang's photographs are beautiful and make us want to see and know more about the people in the portraits. We long for images that portray people as they were and not only as a specter of their former selves.

The portraits of *Forgotten Faces* fulfill that promise. They present photographs of people instead of ghosts, of vibrant faces, not images crumbling from age and decay. The portraits of Holy Cross and Colma's Italian Cemetery present their subjects

The 284-acre Holy Cross Cemetery can be seen at the lower bottom right of San Bruno Mountain just south of San Francisco in this 1999 photograph.

as they lived – postured, happy, engaged, thoughtful, playful, proud and, often, together. These images from the past remain preserved, encapsulated in time and somehow real to us in the present.

From my home on Montara mountain, I returned many times to Holy Cross Cemetery. Each visit brought much information to light. The portraits often came in clusters. Vast expanses of the cemetery contained a sparse few. None of the monuments or mausoleums of the wealthy or well-known were bedecked with these enamel photographs. They were mainly in the immigrant sections of the cemetery's older regions.

My searches turned up more and varied portraits. I found a headstone picture of an entire family, most unusual. In a small patch of the Children's Perpetual Care section I made a dramatic discovery. Postmortem photographs on headstones are now considered rare by some experts; two intact postmortems on a single gravestone are particularly rare. Holy Cross contains two such headstones, each with two postmortem photographs, within 75 feet of each other. A total of seven postmortem portraits were eventually found – all of them children.

Portraits revealing husbands and wives, brothers and sisters and mother and sons also emerged. Most memorial portraits are 3 to 4 inches tall; Holy Cross contained several up to 11 inches in height.

I was also struck by the surprisingly large number of nationalities represented in the portraits. Many came from Southern and Eastern Europe – Italy, France, Switzerland, Austria, Poland and the former Yugoslavia. I also found portraits from Mexico and South America. But the discovery of African Americans, Chinese, Southeast Asians and a Middle Eastern family from the early 20th century in a single cemetery surprised me. The national and ethnic diversity represented by the portraits seemed to mirror San Francisco's immigrant melting pot from a hundred years ago.

Contacts with authorities in the Midwest, on the East Coast, New England and the South revealed helpful insights about photo-ceramic portraits in other areas of the country. The Holy Cross collection of well-preserved portraits was a large one but not the biggest. Its cache of intact postmortem portraits was significant and a valuable reserve of these increasingly rare artifacts. And the broad representation of nations in a single cemetery was unusual and distinctive.

In every geographical location, the portraits are disappearing through vandalism and decay. Many authorities estimated that half were already missing or destroyed in their areas.

Beautiful collections of photo-ceramic memorial portraits from this era exist in many American cities. Yet except for a few dedicated groups and publications, this national heritage lies hidden in history's shadows. These works of art remain forgotten, undocumented and threatened. That is the seed that blossomed into *Forgotten Faces*.

Yet this book will always be about the photographs, the living faces forgotten in the fields of our dead. It is, first and foremost, a book of images – images about people, images about the past, images that suspend us between these two worlds. The accompanying text is meant to help inform, answer questions and provide useful context for the pictures. But mostly the photographs speak for themselves. These faces full of life breach the gap of time and tell their own story. That story is persuasive in and of itself. I encourage you to listen with your eyes wide open.

Color Plates – Holy Cross Cemetery – Favorites

Louise Bajada
1917 — 1928   Age 11

Edna Wolters
1903 — 1928   Age 25   See p. 37

Marko Petrinic
Died Dec. 30th, 1924   Age 28

Sophie Nuby
1887 — 1925   Age 38
Born in Jamaica

Mina Maffei
Died June 21, 1921   Age 19
See p. 46

I

Holy Cross Cemetery

Elvira Russett
1893 — 1926 Age 33

Domitila Padilla
Died May 27, 1921 Age 32

Jose Bermudez
1893 — 1932 Age 39

Frances Bzik
1885 — 1930 Age 45
Born in Yugoslavia

Norbert Maynard Gills
No dates

Holy Cross Cemetery

Joseph D. Warris
1898 —1920 See p.41

See p.41

William Mooney
1874 — 1926   Age 52

Anna Monte
Died August 14, 1934

Grace Costa
1894 —1936

Age 40

Ermine Romomguire
1877 — 1913

Age 36

Holy Cross Cemetery
The Children

George Momsen
1935 — 1937
Age 1 year, 10 months.

Jackie Mulcrevy
Died August 12, 1929
Age 7 years, 8 months.

Elena Moreno Belasco
December 18, 1932
March 19, 1936   Age 4

Carlo M. Carino
1920 — 1921
Age 1 year, 8 months

Alice Portos
1911 —1921   Age 9
See p. 71

Colma's Italian Cemetery
I Bambini

Franko Marciano
Born September 21 1904
Died on his birthday 1909

Alfredo Benugli
1918 — 1922
Age 3 years, 10 months.

Evelina Pinelli
October 4, 1918
July 8, 1929   Age 10

Aurora Grosini
March 17, 1926
March 9, 1927
One year less 8 days

Italia Caseli
December 21, 1924
June 31, 1926

Colma's Italian Cemetery

Anita Amanini

1903 — 1918   Age 15

See p. 104

Maria Belluomini

1889 — 1903

Age 14

Joao M. Aleixo

1884 — 1945

Born in Portugal

Giuseppina Sandroni

1887—1946

Age 59

Salvatore La Rocca

Died February 1, 1920

Age 29   *See p. 114*

Colma's Italian Cemetery

Tana McFadden
November 19, 1900 to April 19, 1925

Giovanni Mordinoia
Died in 1922 at age 23

Paolina Castagno
Born in Airola, Italy April 28, 1889
Died in S.F. June 16, 1914 Age 25

Angela and Giuseppe Balestrieri
Angela died June 27, 1904 Age 49
Giuseppe died Sept. 4, 1914 Age 68

Mrs. Caruso
No date or inscriptions

Colma's Italian Cemetery

Isolina Luchessi
1922 — 1935   Age 13

Giuseppe Bertolino
1896 — 1934   Age 38

Malia Bozzo
1896 — 1918
Age 22

Guilio E. Lazzerini
1921 —1934
Age 13

Giuseppe Grisenti
1897 — 1935
Age 38

Couples from Holy Cross and the Italian Cemetery

Jeanette and Edward Duffy
Jeanette died 1923 age 29, Edward died in 1921 age

Peter and Virginia Fustini
Peter 1882 – 1930, Virgina 1888 — 1954

Frank and Theresa Fazzio
Frank 1902 — 1929 Age 27
Theresa 1905 — 1932 Age 27

Edward and Palmira Banchero
Palmira 1900 — 1929 Age 29
Edward 1886 — 1978 Age 92

Joseph and Cecelia Clement
Joseph died Sept. 29, 1924 Age 35
Cecelia August 6, 1925 Age 32

Tinted Portraits

Josephine Scibuola
1918 — 1941   Age 23

Lucille Verduzco
1923 — 1935   Age 12

Mary Cordtz
November 22, 1862
February 16, 1922   Age 60

Celestina Masotto
Died 1920
Age 3

Louise Franceschini
Died April 16, 1921
Age 38

Stephen Montanarelli
March 21, 1929 to May 14, 2004
To my dad, who died shortly before this book went to press.

CHAPTER TWO

A History of Photographic Tombstones

by Lisa Montanarelli

Photography was invented in the 1830s. It was widespread by the early 1900s, when the people depicted in *Forgotten Faces* had their portraits taken. This technology changed people's lives to such an extent that some claimed it redefined vision. Emile Zola wrote, "We cannot claim to have really seen anything before having photographed it" (Sturken 118). Nineteenth-century viewers were startled by photography's ability to imitate life. This must have been equally startling to early 20th-century immigrants who had never seen a photograph in their homelands.

The advent of photography had three effects that are particularly relevant to memorial portraiture and to *Forgotten Faces*. It facilitated the reproduction of images, made portraiture available to the lower and middle classes, and supplemented people's memory of the past.

A book like *Forgotten Faces* would be impossible without the ability to duplicate and mass-produce images. Before photography, it was difficult to reproduce a work of art, such as a painted portrait. Photography made the process of duplicating images relatively easy. This is essential to memorial portraiture. The photo of the deceased was copied at least twice. The family typically sent a copy of the photo overseas to a European artisan, who made another copy, then fired the image onto an enamel or porcelain surface. The photo-ceramic portrait attached to the gravestone is thus a copy of a copy.

Photography also made portraiture available to the lower and middle classes. As Stanley B. Burns says in *Death in America*, "for the first time in the history of the world, a working class person could have a representation of themselves." In the first decade of the 20th century, Sears-Roebuck advertised photographs set in gravestones: "Imperishable Limoges porcelain portraits preserve the features of the deceased." At "$11.20 for a photograph set in marble, $15.75 for one set in granite," these portraits "competed with the cost of many burial plots" (Jackson and Vergara 46-7). But the prices were cheap compared to the cost of commissioning a painting or sculpture. Memorials reflect class status. Photographic tombstones are primarily a working class phenomenon. Monuments to the rich and famous usually display sculptures rather than photographs.

Because photography offered portraiture to the lower and middle classes, it is often considered democratic. As Jay Ruby points out, the photographers were not intentionally egalitarian. Seeing that portraiture was the most lucrative way for painters to make a living, photographers borrowed the conventions of portraiture from painting and offered the service to a broader market (24).

In *Forgotten Faces*, the photographs of Annie Corcoran (p. 39) and Pauline (p. 144) illustrate how photography borrowed conventions from other arts. Early 20th-century studio portraits often included an image of someone who couldn't be present for the photograph. Annie and Pauline both wear pictures of absent loved ones on their broaches. This convention is called *mise-en-abîme*, the artistic device of placing a play within a play, a story within a story, or in this case, a portrait within a portrait. Paintings sometimes employ this device. But as I mentioned above, it is much easier to take a photograph of another portrait than to reproduce a painting within another painting.

The third way that photography changed people's lives is perhaps the most significant for photo-tombstones. As John Matturi writes in "Windows in the Garden," "Photography… [tends] to elicit an imagined sense of being in contact with the object portrayed" (34n23). Although a photographic portrait, like painted portrait, can be altered and manipulated, a photograph usually appears more lifelike. This gives viewers a sense of nearness to the person portrayed. Elizabeth Barrett commented that photographic portraits conveyed "not merely the likeness" but the "sense of nearness—the very shadow of the person lying there fixed forever" (Matturi 20, 34n24). In 1861 Oliver Wendell Holmes wrote:

> Those whom we love no longer leave us in dying, as they did of old. They remain with us just as they appeared in life; they look down upon us from our walls; they lie upon our tables; they rest upon our bosoms; nay, if we will, we may wear their portraits, like signet-rings, upon our fingers. Our own eyes lose the images pictured on them. Parents sometimes forget the faces of their own children in a separation of a year or two. But the unfading retina which has looked upon them retains their impress, and a fresh beam lays this on the living nerve as if it were radiated from the breathing shape. How these shadows last, and how their originals fade away! (14)

The invention of photography shocked mid-19th-century viewers. Its lifelike qualities made it especially suitable for supplementing memory and memorializing the dead. As Burns says, "the photograph allowed the family to have a visual memory of the person. It served the purpose of pushing the dead away—which is something we must do when someone dies—yet keeping them with us." Hence the frequent placement of photographs on the tombstones of infants and children: "Parents sometimes forget the faces of their own children in a separation of a year or two."

One can give numerous examples of how people use photographs to supplement memory. In court cases, attorneys present photos as evidence of how crimes were committed. Parents photograph their children to remember how they looked at different ages, and people take photographs at family reunions to show how many relatives gathered in the same place at the same time.

The use of a photograph as evidence or as an aid to memory is deceptive because a photograph can be manipulated or falsified to show something that never happened. We usually associate these modifications with computer graphics (airbrushing an ex-boyfriend out of a family picture or adding people to a landscape they never visited), but the possibility of manipulating images has been with photography since its inception.

Retouching has always been an integral part of memorial portraiture. In this sense, memorial portraiture anticipates the manipulations of digital photography. Artisans frequently retouched the portraits to present the subject in a more flattering light or to remove another person from the picture. Louise Bajada's portrait was retouched to conceal a hand on Louise's shoulder and the dress of a woman standing behind her (p. 16, color portrait, p. I). Artisans also retouched snapshots to make the image suitable for display in a cemetery. A contemporary memorial portrait maker describes how he alters photographs according to the family's specifications: "People have their hair chopped off, or hold a drink in their hand or are standing on a beach wearing a bathing suit. The family wants us to put a coat and tie on them—we can do that, and we can also remove bottles, drinks and cigarettes" (Jackson and Vergara 47).

Memorial portraits were also retouched to sharpen the image. As mentioned above, a ceramic photograph attached to the tombstone is a copy of a copy. The family held on to the photo and sent a copy to the artisan, who made another copy before burning the image onto enamel or porcelain. By the time it was fired in the kiln, the image had been copied so many times that its sharpness had been lost.

Artisans also retouched the photographs because they knew that the images would fade after years outdoors in the sun. They outlined and sharpened the images so that the features of the person's face would remain visible for a longer period of time. Unfortunately, after many decades some photographs vanish completely so that only the craftsman's drawings remain.

In *Mount Zion Sepulchral Portraits,* John Yang explores how these retouchings sometimes outlast the photographic image. Twentieth-century advertisements promised that photo-ceramics were absolutely permanent, but many portraits have been vandalized or faded beyond recognition. *Mount Zion Sepulchral Portraits* presents Yang's photographs of damaged portraits from Mount Zion Cemetery, located in Maspeth, Queens. Though Mount Zion houses many well-preserved photo-ceramics, Yang focuses his lens on the worn and vandalized portraits, including some that are so faded that the retouchings—the artisans' manipulations—are more visible than the photographic image.

In contrast to *Mount Zion Sepulchral Portraits, Forgotten Faces* focuses on portraits in excellent condition. Though many of these portraits have also been retouched, the artisan's handiwork is less obvious. In the portrait of Louise Bajada, one can barely discern the obliterated hand on Louise's shoulder. Some of the most interesting manipulations are the amalgams of two or more photographs, as in the images of Ermanno and Declinda Parensi (p. 163), Teresa and Giuseppe Musante, and Liesl and Meinrad Eberhard (p. 49). Some memorial portraits combine images of relatives who lived at different times and in different places in order to give the family an effect of historical continuity. As I discuss in chapter five, this desire for historical continuity partly explains why photo-tombstones were popular among immigrants, who wanted to maintain a strong sense of cultural identity and familial continuity even though they were separated from their homeland and from their loved ones.

Since Ron Horne describes enamel photography in Chapter Four, I will focus on the early history of photographic tombstones. Americans have attached photos to tombstones since the invention of the daguerreotype. The most famous daguerreotype stone, located in Oak Hill Cemetery in Washington, D.C., displays the image of "Nephi Bell, who died November 22nd, 1862, aged 19 years, 2 months, 17 days." Ruby writes: "based on news items in 19th-century photographic magazines and journals and the number of patents registered for devices for securing photographs to tombstones, it is evident that [photographic tombstones] existed from the 1840s onward" (Ruby 143).

Ruby cites numerous references to daguerreotypes on tombstones. It is worth recording some of these references for those who are interested. On November 29, 1853, The Pittsburgh Morning Post ran this item: "A grave-stone… has at the top a daguerreotype of the deceased person, neatly set into the stone. This is a novel and appropriate method, not only of commemorating friends, but of bringing them, as they appeared in life, to the recollection of acquaintances visiting their graves" (Ruby 143).

On May 11, 1857 *Hutching's Illustrated California Magazine* published an anonymous article, "Daguerreotypes on Tombstones": "If on every tombstone there

New York's Mt. Zion Cemetery contains hundreds of photo-ceramic memorial portraits from the early twentieth century from those of Eastern European Jewish descent.

Photos by Lisa Montanarelli

could be seen the life-likeness of the sleeper… how much more inviting would then be the last resting place of the departed—could we thus seek the 'living' among the 'dead' and on every tombstone see the living representative of the sleeper" (Ruby 145-6).

An article from the November 3, 1907 *Indianapolis Sunday Star* describes a local doctor, Oliver F. Fitch, placing a daguerreotype on his wife's tombstone in 1853:

> The grief-stricken husband placed a slab of pure Italian marble at her grave and in it he set the girlhood picture of his young wife. Since the death of Mrs. Fitch, in 1853, the picture has faced storm and sunshine unprotected, and yet the hand of love had done its work so well that the picture may be copied today by any ordinary camera. (Ruby 146)

Other documents record patents and "improvements" in daguerrean tombstones. The inventors' main concern was how to make the photographs last longer, since photos are less durable than stone. On March 11, 1851 Solon Jenkins, Jr. of West Cambridge, Massachusetts, obtained the first known patent for "Securing Daguerreotypes on Monumental Stones." U.S. Patent No. 7974 states that Jenkins had invented "a peculiar mode of attaching, permanently and durably, a daguerreotype or photographic portrait to an ordinary monumental stone" (Rinhart and Rinhart 304). *Scientific American* reports two improvements for attaching daguerreotypes to monuments in the September 9, 1954 issue (410) and the January 5, 1856 issue (136). The next patent went to N.W. Langley, Henry Jones, and Aaron S. Drake on December 6, 1859 (U.S. Patent No. 26, 370).

Despite the number of patents and news articles, few 19th-century photo tombstones are known in the United States. This explains the scarcity of postmortem photos on gravestones. Postmortems were common in the 19th century, but by the 20th century, they were no longer considered publicly acceptable.

As Ruby notes, the lack of 19th-century photo tombstones presents something of a mystery:

> The number of patents and companies offering the service and the amount of discussion in the photographic trade journals certainly supports the notion that the practice was widespread. Where these stones are remains a mystery.... there is no evidence that any of the entrepreneurs mentioned ever manufactured or sold any of these devices... It would seem logical to assume that if all of the inventors described... saw photographic tombstones as potential moneymakers, then there must have been a considerable market. (153, 169)

Most of the 19th-century photo tombstones may have been damaged or vandalized. When touring cemeteries, one occasionally sees stones with empty glass cases, which may have contained a daguerreotype. Some cemeteries simply remove damaged stones. Monuments of the wealthy have trust funds for maintenance and repair, but photo tombstones are mostly a working class phenomenon. Most families can't afford to keep up a gravestone indefinitely, and in the case of a 19th-century tombstone, everyone who knew the person has died.

Because the photographs are prone to vandalism, some cemeteries prohibit photographic tombstones. Most of these rules went into effect in the 1940s. Since September 1942, Catholic cemeteries in Philadelphia have enforced the following rule: "Photographs of any kind, or other representations of the person interred, are not permitted on cemetery plots or on memorials in the cemeteries."[14] When Ruby inquired about these prohibitions, he received the following response from the Executive Director, National Catholic Cemetery Conference:

"There is no uniformity on whether or not such photographs are permitted in a

---

[14] *Rules and Regulations of Philadelphia Diocesan Cemeteries* (Philadelphia: Catholic Cemeteries Office, n.d.), cited in Ruby 146, 197n6.

Catholic cemetery. Cemeterians who do not permit these in their cemeteries inform me that the major reason is vandalism. If the pictures are damaged and destroyed, the remaining monument is unsightly—thus, the prohibiting of permitting such photos. I can inform you that the majority of Catholic cemeteries (both diocesan operated and parish operated) do not permit such photos in their cemeteries."[15]

Catholic cemeteries are not alone in forbidding these memorials. Mount Zion, the Jewish cemetery where Yang took his photos, no longer permits them, and Ruby notes: "Laurel Gabel informs me that the New London Cemetery (Connecticut) and Cedar Grove Cemetery (Iowa) both have regulations: 'Photographic reproductions of the deceased on gravestones are forbidden'" (197n7).

While most cemeteries claim vandalism as their reason for outlawing memorial portraits, John Matturi gives a different reason: the pressure to assimilate. As I discuss in chapter five, photographic tombstones were most common among immigrants from Southern and Eastern Europe, who brought this custom from their homelands. According to Matturi, the prohibitions in Catholic cemeteries may be a "manifestation of the longstanding disapproval that the predominantly Northern European American Catholic hierarchy felt toward the popular religion and culture of Southern European immigrants" (30). This isn't surprising since, for most of the 20th century, American culture denied the reality of death and frowned upon overt displays of grief. In this sense, the presence of photo tombstones in the United States shows the strength with which immigrants clung to their customs in an often hostile new world.

[15] Ruby 146, personal communication from Leo A. Droste, C.A.E., Executive Director, National Catholic Cemetery Conference, January 5, 1993.

Works Cited

Burns, Stanley B. Executive Producer. *Death in America: A Chronological History of Illness and Death*. Produced and directed by J.R. Olivero. Black Mirror Films, 1998.

Carpenter, Woodrow. Enamel Photography. Society of Dutch Enamellers. http://www.enamellers.nl/english/carpenter1.htm

Holmes, Oliver Wendell. 1861. Sun-Painting and Sun-Sculpture. In *Atlantic Monthly* 8 (July).

Jackson, Kenneth and Camilo José Vergara. 1989. *Silent Cities*. New York: Princeton Architectural Press.

Matturi, John. 1993. Windows in the Garden: Italian-American Memorialization and the American Cemetery. In *Ethnicity and the American Cemetery*. Edited by Richard E. Meyer. Bowling Green, Ohio: Bowling Green State University Popular Press, 14-35.

Rinehart, Floyd and Marion Rinehart. 1980. *The American Daguerreotype*. Athens: University of Georgia Press.

Ruby, Jay. 1995. *Secure the Shadow: Death and Photography in America*. Cambridge and London: MIT Press.

Sturken, Marita and Lisa Cartwright. 2001. *Practices of Looking: An Introduction to Visual Culture*. New York: Oxford University Press.

Yang, John. *Mount Zion Sepulchral Portraits*. 2001. New York: D.A.P/Distributed Art Publishers, Inc.

Photo-Gallery I

The Portraits of Holy Cross Cemetery I

The Domachin Angel marks the entrance to the Slavonic section of Holy Cross which contains one of the highest concentrations of portraits in the cemetery. Holy Cross is the largest and oldest cemetery in Colma, California known as the City of Cemeteries. Established in 1867, Holy Cross covers 283 acres of forested rolling hills at the foot of San Bruno Mountain. It currently contains almost 300,000 interments. Memorial portraits from the early 20th century come in clusters, sometimes related to nationality. Large sections contain only isolated portraits from this era. Some portraits are still being discovered today.

The Unresolved Murder of Bridget Kearney 1904—1928

Bridie's Story

Bridie Kearney was shot to death while attending a wedding celebration on Sutter Street in San Francisco. She was 24 years old. Witnesses at the wedding party identified Lloyd Groat, a San Francisco policeman, as having fired the shot that killed Ms. Kearney. They agreed that Bridie was leaving the hall with her brother Patrick, fiancé John Keane and other guests when she was shot through the temple. Keane received a flesh-wound in the forehead from the same bullet. The gun was found in the gutter with a single shot fired missing from its empty chamber.

Bridie's sister, Betty Kearney, told reporters "they will try to cover this up. I know they will." She was in the hall at the time of the shooting.

During the course of the trial, witnesses often contradicted each other whether as to Office Groat actually fired his gun. He claimed the gun was taken from his holster in a struggle and he never held it in his hand. When other witnesses recanted original testimony regarding Groat, he was acquitted of the crime and instructed to report back to duty. There were no other suspects and no one was ever convicted of the shooting.

Officer Groat returned to work only to retire from the force four months later without explanation. He was subsequently arrested twice in 1929 for possession of liquor which was still illegal under prohibition. Bridie's murder was never solved. See Bridie's full story on page 121.

Headlines from the archives
of the *San Francisco Chronicle* and *Examiner*
February 27, 1928 to May 22, 1928

Traffic Officer, Skull Crushed, Found in Street

Believed to Have Fallen With Motorcycle While Pursuing Automobile

Benjamin G. Root   1898—1926
See Officer Root's full story on page 123.

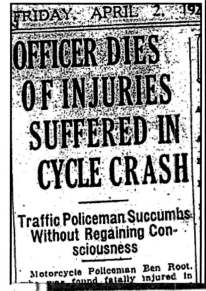

FRIDAY, APRIL 2, 192_

OFFICER DIES OF INJURIES SUFFERED IN CYCLE CRASH

Traffic Policeman Succumbs Without Regaining Consciousness

Motorcycle Policeman Ben Root was found fatally injured in

One Ray of Sunshine

FUND SOARS FOR FAMILY OF POLICEMAN

As Hundreds Attend Funeral, Many Express Sympathy for Bereaved With Contributions

Mrs. Helen Root and a check for $1,275, which was donated to her by "Examiner" readers, and son James. Mrs Root's husband, a traffic policeman, was killed while on duty

Pvt. James Kendrick, World War I Veteran
"Died May 25, 1919, Age 21 years
Member Co. H.363rd INF. .A.E.F. France"
See Pvt. Kendrick's full story on page 122.

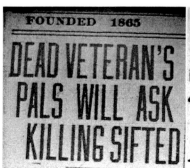

FOUNDED 1865

DEAD VETERAN'S PALS WILL ASK KILLING SIFTED

Remains of James Kendrick, Shot by Policeman, Viewed by 1000 Men of 363d

FUNERAL HELD YESTERDAY

"It Wouldn't Be Bad to Die in Action," Says Friend, "but Finished by a Cop——"

POLICEMAN WHO SHOT KENDRICK HELD TO BLAME

Coroner's Jury Demands That Kelly Face Jury for Manslaughter

TESTIMONY CONFLICTING

Slayer Says Former Soldier Showed Fight; Friends Refute His Story

34

In the Line of Duty

Florence Font *1897—1924*
Nurse Age 27

Anthony Mello *1892—1921*
Fireman Age 29

John Govednick *1887—1930*
WWI "PVT. Battery F. 37ᵗʰ F.A.
Regiment U.S.A". Age 43

Ivan Blazic *1892—1911*
"Unforgettable Brother," from Istra, Russia
He was 19 when he died.

The Garry Family
Amy, Celia, Edward and Gertrude
"Our Beloved Daughter Amy 21 years," 1924
Celia 1912—1943;   Edward 1874—1944;   Gertrude 1878—1963

Complete family photographs are rarely used as memorial portraits. Here the Garry family is posed in a studio with a bench and beach scene backdrop. Their hats indicate they may have been visiting an ocean vacation spot where such photographs were offered with a studio reconstruction of the local scenes. The oldest daughter rests her hand on her sister who in turn extends her arm across her father's shoulder.

Edna Wolters
1903 to 1928

Edna poses with an ostrich feather while looking back into the camera's eye with a natural and engaging smile. What did her loved ones want us to know about Edna through the use of this distinctive portrait? Was she an entertainer, a dancer? Her portrait makes us want to know more even as it tells us more than we could ever have known. She died at age 25.

Marko's leg was buried 21 years before the rest of him. His portrait tells his story.

His gravestone tendered only this one-word epitaph, but research reveals he is Harold Rothstein who died in 1920 at age 7.

Mary Heney, who died in 1913 at age 33, and Margaret Brodie, who died in 1919 at age 28 share this two-word epitaph.

The ceramic portrait on the right was badly fractured but well repaired.

Annie Corcoran

"Died Feb. 22, 1925   Age 87 years   In Memory of Our Mother"
Some portraits include an image of someone who couldn't be present for the photograph. Notice the portrait within the portrait. Annie wears a photo of an absent loved one on her brooch. The term for this process is mise-en-abime.

Ethnic Diversity at Holy Cross

In the early 1900s, memorial portraiture remained most common among immigrants from southern and eastern Europe and Latin America. Unusually diverse, the portraits of Holy Cross include African-Americans and immigrants from China and the Philippines.

Grace Costa   1894—1936

Tajonera   *"Sacred to Peter"*   1893—1922   *Native of the Philippines*

Howard Lee   *1911—1942   Age 31*

Sophie Nuby   *1887—1925   Born in Jamaica.*

40

Men and Women of the Portraits

Joseph D. Warris
September 3, 1898 to February 28, 1920
Joseph's father, Kalil, is a native of Syria. His mother, Philomena, is from Lebanon.
Portraits from descendents of the Middle East are uncommon during this era.

Fashions of the Age

Anthony wears an overlapping lapel typical of late nineteenth century men's fashion.

Age 15 in 1928, Constance sports bobbed hair and a low-waisted belt from the Roaring Twenties.

Anthony O'Brien   1860—1899

Constance Mora

Math Judnich
1887—1940
Compare Math's attire with Rico's more conservative style.

Rico Nitrio, *19 in 1931, poses ready for business in a knotted Windsor, overcoat and brushed felt hat.*

Catherine Elich

July 9, 1905 — December 25, 1927
Catherine wears cropped hair and a full fur —
distinct Roaring Twenties fashion.

Elvira Russett

1893 — 1926
Elvira displays a curl in the middle of her forehead
and a gossamer gown from the mid-twenties.

Brigette Sans   *1877 — 1928*
Brigette wears high-necked lace
from the early 1900s.

Stefina Tocker   *1905 — 1934*
Stefina boasts a white fur collar with pearls and
holds a purse in her right hand.

Marko Petrinic

Born 1894, died December 30, 1924   "Rest Dear Husband"
Marko's studio portrait was taken for a special occasion. With lighting from his upper right to highlight his best features, this photo represents classic portraiture style. Marko's eyes look away from the camera as if into the future. He offers us an interesting hairstyle as well.

The Gracieux Sisters: Maria and Antonita

October 18, 1905 – April 3, 1919

January 23, 1903 – May 25, 1910

The Gracieux sisters' flowered cross lies at a remote edge of the cemetery. The worn inscription reads, "In Memory of My Loving Daughters." Antonita (above right) died at age 7 in 1910. Maria (left), kneeling for her First Holy Communion, died in 1919 at age 13.

Below: the distant northern corner of Holy Cross where the stone of the Gracieux sisters has stood for over ninety years.

Cut Before the Bloom

In our sample of 500 portraits, two out of every three subjects died before reaching the age 30.

Defendante Guerra
1906 — 1927
"Defender of War"

Liberante Terranova
1905 — 1924
"Liberator of the New World"

Bessie Wong
1901 — 1924

Mina A. Maffei

Bessie's portrait is signed, probably by the photographer, "S.Tou" in the lower right.

"Died June 29, 1921 age 19 years"
Mina's formal portrait bears the inscription of the photography studio "La Fayette S.F" in the lower right.

Jules
1875—1912   Age 37

Julie
1879—1912   Age 33

The Fourgous Family ▶

Jules and Julie Fourgous immigrated to the United States from France. Jules died in May of 1912. Julie died in November of the same year. Their son Fernand, orphaned at 13, survived only to the age of 26 and died in 1925.

The Perez Family

Salena (left) died at age 18 in December, 1915, her sister Lucy (right), age 17 in December, 1919. Their mother Marie (center) died in 1922 at age 50. Father Theodore died in 1935 at age 66. Notice how the casual snapshots of the Perez sisters contrast with the studio portraits of the Fourgous. ▼

Fernand
1899—1925   Age 26

Selena

Maria

Lucy

Livia Corlin
"Died February 4, 1932 at 16 years"
Livia's portrait reveals a wedding ring on her left hand signifying she married prior to her death at 16. Her portrait comes from the Holy Cross cemetery in Palo Alto, California.

Giuseppe's mother died when he
was seven. He lived five more years.

Teresa and Giuseppe Musante
Died April 14, 1920   Died March 29, 1925

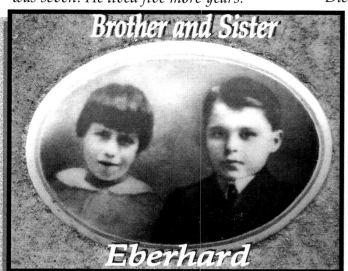

Liesel
Eberhard
age 11
(left)

Meinrad
Eberhard
age 17
(right)

"Our Beloved
Children"

Zacarias
Martinez

1880 to
Dec. 3, 1924

Concepcion
Martinez

1880 to
Dec. 16, 1924

Dorothy Kristolovich
January 4, 1901—April 20, 1929
Her son Joseph "Born and died on April 20, 1929."
The story of Dorothy and her son Joseph is told in the details of their epitaph.
She is pictured here wearing her wedding dress.

CHAPTER THREE

The Significance of the Holy Cross Memorial Portrait Collection

Three principal attributes define the photo-ceramic memorial portraits of Holy Cross Cemetery as a distinctive and important representation of the art form.

First, Holy Cross contains at least 500 well-preserved portraits from the early 20th century, ranking it one of the larger cemeteries in the country in sheer numbers of the portraits.

Holy Cross also shelters seven postmortem portraits. That's a significant number. Some industry experts now consider postmortem photographs still intact on tombstones as rare[2]. All the Holy Cross postmortems are of children. Death rates among children were so high during this era that postmortems of the very young were "often the only images ever captured of their subjects."[3] These portraits sometimes represent the only picture of that child still in existence.

Jay Ruby, author of *Secure the Shadow – Death and Photography in America,* tells us that today a single tombstone containing two postmortem photographs can be considered "doubly rare." Holy Cross contains two such headstones. These intact postmortem portraits alone make Holy Cross an important anthropological reserve of these valued artifacts.

Lastly, its memorial portraits represent 28 different nationalities. This makes Holy Cross unusually diverse for a single cemetery. It yields particularly hard-to-find ethnicities from the early 20th century, including African Americans, Chinese, South East Asians, South Americans and the Middle East.

Such a broad representation of so many nations and cultures is uncommon in a single-denominational cemetery. Midwestern and East Cost cemeteries often categorize themselves by nationality or religion such as Lithuanian, Bohemian, German, Italian, Jewish, Catholic or Lutheran. Finding so many different nations represented in one cemetery is unusual.

African American portraits from this era are relatively rare; Holy Cross contains two. Though the Chinese have readily adopted memorial portraiture in the modern era, they are seldom found from the early 1900s; Holy Cross contains three. South East Asians are quite uncommon; Holy Cross has two. Middle

---

[2] Jay Ruby, Author of *Secure the Shadow: Death and Photography in America*

[3] Dr. Stanley B. Burns, *Death in America*

TABLE 1 - National Origins of Holy Cross Portraits

(listing is limited to one to three names to preserve space)

1. **Austria** – Marko Franciskovich, Marko Petrinic, Judnich
2. **Chile** – Custodio Silva
3. **China** – Howard Lee, Bessie Wong
4. **Croatia** – Antic Jakov, Ivan Kriletic, Reparata Lupich
5. **Czechoslovakia** – Vukovich Ignacio
6. **England** – Mary May Green, Henry Stratton
7. **France** – Louise and Antonin Garaudel, Fourgous family
8. **Germany** – Bertha Beuhler, Eberhard family
9. **Hungary** – Rosie Rauchau
10. **Ireland** – James Dunleavy, Bridie Kearney, Bridie Murphy
11. **Italy** – Lydia Vanucci, Luigi Scafani
12. **Jamaica** – Sophie Nuby
13. **Lithuania** – John and Mary Mordus, parents of Helen and Ellen
14. **Malta** – Angela/Joseph Grech, John Sherry
15. **Mexico** – Mercedes DeLira Smith, Lupe Vera, Guadelupe Zazueta
16. **Philippines, South East Asia** – Luciano Desquites, Tajonera Peter
17. **Poland** – Garaslmowicz, Mary and Nancy
18. **Portugal** – Antonio Viera
19. **Romania** – Joseph Mareck
20. **Russia** – Ivan Blazic
21. **San Salvador** – Victor Montalvo
22. **Scotland** – Edward Heatson
23. **Serbia** – Joseph Puzina
24. **Slovenia** – Joseph Gersich
25. **Spain** – Annie and Manuel Monte
26. **Switzerland** – Defendente Guerra, Christine Ettlin, Rosa Portman
27. **Ukraine** – Miho Vilcevich
28. **Yugoslavia** – Francis Bzik

Eastern portraits from this era are also scarce; there's one at Holy Cross.

As do many Catholic cemeteries, Holy Cross contains a rich representation of European immigrants and first-generation descendants. This unusually broad national representation, detailed in Table 1, sets Holy Cross apart.

The sizable number of well-preserved portraits, the significant quantity of rare portraits and the broad national diversity — combine to make Holy Cross a significant representation of this funerary art.

Its intact postmortem reserve further enhances its importance as a sanctuary of these valued relics. Ultimately, the Holy Cross collection of well-preserved memorial portraits presents an outstanding example of the art form and is one of the more diverse single-cemetery collections in the nation.

Colma's Italian Cemetery

If Holy Cross stands out for its diversity, Colma's Italian Cemetery (p. 94) represents the art form at its highest evolutionary point, gracing the graves of the deceased from the country most responsible for popularizing and perfecting the art. Containing approximately 800 well-preserved portraits from the early 20th century, the Italian Cemetery offers greater numbers than Holy Cross; however, its ethnic representation is understandably more limited. The Italian Cemetery allows a significant number of interments of Spanish and Latin Americans as well as a few other nationalities. But it is dominated by those of Italian descent. The Italians have valued and enhanced the art of memorial portraiture since its inception. They are widely credited with popularizing photo-ceramic memorial portraiture throughout Southern Europe and the United States.

As the Italians migrated to the United States in the 1830s first, and then in 1900's third wave[4] of immigrants, they fostered this tradition wherever they lived and died. Their widespread use of photo-ceramic portraits led to its continuing refinement. Italian portraits contain creative and elaborate family composites, sumptuous imagery and historically interesting details. Lisa Montanarelli adds, "Their interpretations of the art reflect the culture's deep reverence for its ancestry and the honor they convey by the longevity of their family's images."

The Italian Cemetery also contains at least seven confirmed postmortems. More may exist, subject to verification. One is that of an adult. That distinguishes it from Holy Cross with seven postmortems, all of children. Like most

---

[4] Joyce Bryant – Yale-New Haven Teacher's Institute *Immigration in the United States*

cemeteries, the Italian Cemetery does not contain any tombstones with more than one postmortem portrait. Holy Cross remains distinctive in that regard.

However, the Italian Cemetery postmortems are notable for the postmortem portrait (p. 115) of the twin children of the Baiocchi family - Gino and Aldo. The author has not been able to confirm any funerary expert who has ever seen a postmortem portrait of twins on a tombstone. The Baiocchi portrait can be considered quite rare; possibly one of a kind. Gino and Aldo were both born on July 5, 1928 and died eleven months later and three days apart on June 2nd and May 31st respectively. Along with the other six confirmed postmortems, including one adult, the assemblage of postmortems portraits found at the Italian Cemetery represent an extremely valuable and important reserve of these rare artifacts.

The Italian Cemetery possesses the portrait of one veteran from America's Civil War. Giuseppe Garbone (p. 100) was 16 at the time of the conflict. The photo of him wearing a Grand Army of the Republic insignia, uniform and veteran's medals was taken when he was much older – possibly attending a GAR reunion. The cemetery also contains memorial portraits of veterans from WWI and WWII (including a woman in uniform) as well as those in early Italian military and police uniforms. Its representation of uniformed subjects is large and varied.

In Colma's Italian Cemetery one walks from one tombstone to the next examining memorial portraits on every other stone. They are virtually everywhere you look. Many stones contain family portraits from several generations. Frequently the photographs used for memorials are studio-produced portraits with elaborate, symbolic props and exotic backgrounds that convey an other-worldly quality. The portraits are also sometimes signed by the original photographer as in the example of Emelio Baldocchi on page 105. The photographer's signature, L.Tagliano, can also found on other portraits in the Italian Cemetery.

Small, gated and located in a highly visible slice of the city of Colma, the Italian Cemetery is less a target of vandalism than most, though it is still pocked with the many empty oval shapes that once contained a valued portrait mounted on the stone.

The Italian Cemetery has one of the larger caches of photo-ceramic memorial portraiture in America. It contains several rare postmortem portraits still intact. And its memorial portraiture possesses a degree of cultural refinement and artistic elegance that befits the nation most responsible for its development and maturity as an art form.

Photo-Ceramic Memorial Portraiture in the United States

Memorial portraits receive little popular attention. *Forgotten Faces* is the first book to systematically survey and document a large urban cemetery environment – Colma, California – for well-preserved memorial portraits from the early 20th century. No other such survey exists. No documentation or accurate count of intact portraits remaining in the major historical U.S. cities has ever been undertaken. This lack of information makes it hard to compare the Colma cemeteries' collections with those elsewhere.

Reliable anecdotal information from informed local authorities has proven our most useful resource. The following conclusions are based on these sources, Internet searches, industry associations and publications on specific cemeteries.

Holy Cross' well-preserved examples often present photographic detail as perfect as the day their image was captured. But are the 500 intact portraits there typical of a large urban cemetery? How do they compare in quality and quantity with the portraits from this era in cemeteries elsewhere?

From discussions with informed sources, published cemetery information and predictive extrapolations, I estimate that between 25,000 and 35,000 well-preserved photo-ceramic memorial portraits from the early 20th century still exist in the roughly 1,500 urban cemeteries in the United States.

The very largest cemeteries contain from 800 to 1,000 photo-ceramic portraits from the era. Mount Carmel and others in Chicago may have more. The larger caches, as found in Colma's Holy Cross and Italian cemeteries, number between 500 and 800. Cemeteries such as New York's Mount Zion, Philadelphia's Holy Cross, Savannah's Bonaventure and Oakland's St. Mary's define a mid-tier profile possessing 200 to 500 memorial portraits from the early 20th century.

Most cemeteries have fewer than 100, including Colma's Greek Orthodox and Serbian cemeteries as well as many in Northern California's rural burial grounds such as Roseville, north of Sacramento. Of course, many cemeteries, even ones over 100 years old, but especially those with nondenominational charters, contain none at all from this period. In the capital of California, Sacramento's Old City Cemetery, established in 1849, contains the graves of many famous pioneers including Johann Sutter Jr., Mark Hopkins, Edwin Crocker and several Donner party survivors. However no memorial portraits from this era have been located. Its notable lack of these artifacts reinforces the ethnic origins and tradition of memorial portraiture.

Comparing the Holy Cross Collection

Comparing Holy Cross with its Colma neighbors helps define its significance locally.

The Italian Cemetery reflects its nation's rich tradition in memorial portraiture. Its scant 40 acres with over 50,000 interments yields approximately 800 well-preserved portraits from this early era, 32 portraits per acre.

Holy Cross, by contrast, is more than 10 times larger and contains vast areas with very few portraits from that time. With 500 portraits, it yields fewer than two portraits per acre. They are most often found concentrated in areas with specific ethnicities and older graves.

These per-acre figures may seem low. Two portraits per acre is not a lot, especially considering some sections contain scores within yards of each other. This numerical skew is due to differences in population from one era to the next. Cemeteries often possess much more densely populated sections, the result of interments from the latter half of the 20th century. Even in the oldest cemeteries, burials from 1900 to 1945 often represent much less than 50% of total cemetery acreage because the population was so much smaller then. In 1900, the U.S. population was 76 million; by 1950, it had doubled to 151 million, and in 2004 it has almost doubled again, reaching 292 million. This 4-to-1 ratio of new graves to old explains why cemeteries contain so much more acreage dedicated to burials after 1940. Further multiply that ratio with the fact that only a minor percentage of headstones from that era contain portraits and the low per acre counts make more sense.

Of the other 15 cemeteries in Colma, none contains more than 50-60 portraits from this period. This includes the celebrated Cypress Lawn Cemetery with 143 acres and 150,000 interments. Cypress Lawn possesses an extensive population of imposing mausoleums representing some of the most affluent and renowned figures from California's past including William Randolph Hearst, Charles DeYoung and Lillie Hitchcock Coit. Yet it is nondenominational and contains fewer than 50 intact portraits, and these are found primarily in one isolated section of its grounds.

The same is true in Oakland, home to California's eminent Mountain View Cemetery that has 165,000 interments on 220 acres. The monuments and mausoleums of the affluent and famous populate the hilly property whose stunning views of San Francisco Bay attract visitors, hikers and family picnickers throughout the year. Yet its nondenominational grounds contain fewer than 50 photo-ceramic portraits from the early 20th century.

Mountain View's next-door neighbor, Saint Mary's Catholic cemetery, again reveals the ethnic traditions behind the portraits. As a Catholic cemetery established in 1863, it contains 80,000 interments on 80 acres. With many early 19th century immigrants from Southern Europe, Saint Mary's yields approximately 300 memorial portraits from this era, an average of 21/2 per acre – close to Holy Cross. Here, too, they appear in clusters; some sections contain many portraits, others very few. St. Mary's used to have many more portraits, but, typically, large numbers are missing from their headstones.

Definitive comparisons of Holy Cross' portrait count with large urban cemeteries remains a challenge. No other major city has ever been surveyed; however, some useful conclusions can be formed from knowledgeable regional sources and gravestone studies.

Chicago – the Cemetery Capital

Chicago's cemetery system, with its Midwest melting pot history, dwarfs all other U.S. cities with more than 200 cemeteries and 5 million total interments for a city with a population of 3 million. By comparison, New York City and environs, with a population of 10 million-plus, has fewer than 100 cemeteries with approximately 2 million interments – a more typical urban ratio. The Los Angeles area offers about 100 cemeteries in LA county and adjacent areas with approximately 2 to 2.5 million interments. The Washington-Baltimore area can claim roughly 50 cemeteries with 1 million to 2 million interments.

Most other large urban areas from the East to the South provide comparisons with San Francisco. Boston, Atlanta, Cleveland, Baltimore, Cincinnati, Charlotte, Raleigh, Miami, Dallas and New Orleans parallel San Francisco's profile with fewer than 30 cemeteries and from 500,000 to 1 million interments within 50 miles of city central.

So it is Chicago that can be accurately named the memorial portrait capital of the United States. Chicago contains many large cemeteries, both in acreage and interments, dedicated to specific nationalities and ethnicities such as Bohemian and

Lithuanian, German and many others, including Middle Eastern cemeteries. They also group burial grounds by religion – Catholic, Jewish, Lutheran and others, as is common in most regions.

Most importantly, Chicago is the U.S. manufacturing capital for memorial portraits with the oldest (1893) U.S. manufacturer, J.A. Dedouch, and Oak Park Monuments, once a part of Dedouch, representing a strong influence on the availability and cultural acceptance of the tradition. Memorial portraits manufactured by Dedouch and Oak Park Monuments are found throughout the vast cemetery grounds of the Chicago vicinity.

Chicago quite likely contains more well-preserved memorial portraits from the early 20th century than anywhere else in the country. Several cemeteries in Chicago contain many hundreds of portraits from this era. Matt Hucke, author of *Graveyards of Chicago: The People, History, Art, and Lore of Cook County Cemeteries*, believes Chicago's Mount Carmel (Italian) and Jewish Waldheim each contain 500 or more portraits from this era.

Mount Carmel also includes the fascinating grave of Julia Buccola Petta, "The Italian Bride," whose two portraits on her impressive monument reveal a fascinating story. Her first portrait shows her wearing her wedding dress. It is mounted next to a postmortem photo portrait taken of her when she was exhumed and moved six years after her death. Some claim that little or no decomposition occurred to Mrs. Petta during her six years underground. You can decide for yourself and observe Julia's one-of-a-kind portraits at www.ItalianAncestry.com/MtCarmel.

Helen Sclair, Chicago's "Cemetery Lady" who has explored, studied and gathered artifacts from Chicago's vast cemetery grounds for decades, believes that Mount Carmel and other cemeteries yield well over 500 portraits from this era, even as many as 1,000. A regular contributor to the *Bulletin of the Association of Gravestone Studies*, she witnessed the numerous postmortems that used to exist in the area. She has verified their subsequent loss and apparent theft. Helen, who actually lives in a cemetery and has an renowned collection of funerary artifacts, confirms the large numbers and great ethnic representation of the Chicago cemeteries.

It is estimated there are between 5,000-7,000 well-preserved photo-ceramic portraits in the Chicago area, though none of it is documented in any organized way.

Several excellent examples of Chicago's treasured art, including a rare postmortem portrait of a nun, are included in *Forgotten Faces* and can be found in the section "Examples of the Art - From the Photo-Archives of Richard Meyer."

Next to Chicago, New York City and surrounding counties incorporate almost 100 cemeteries with approximately two million interments. No organized survey of photo-ceramic portraits has ever been conducted in New York, either.

John Yang's work in Mount Zion Jewish Cemetery was the first to explore the art. Mark Stempa, president of Mount Zion, believes it contains 200 to 300 well-preserved enameled portraits, primarily of Eastern European descent. It is likely, considering the enormous ethnic diversity of the area, that thousands of these portraits exist in New York and vicinity, unnoticed, uncounted and undocumented.

In the country's sixth-largest urban area, Philadelphia's Holy Cross Catholic Cemetery contains several hundred portraits, principally from the 1920s, in very good condition. They are virtually all of Italian origin.

In the Southern United States, Jerry Fleming, director of Savannah, Ga.'s Bonaventure Cemetery estimates that the historic grounds possess "perhaps a hundred or so" portraits. They are found primarily in its Jewish and Italian sections.

New Orleans' celebrated cemeteries are said to harbor hundreds of portraits from this era. The southern part of the United States represents one of the most popular areas of the country for orders of modern memorial portraits from U.S. manufacturers. Richard Meyer has confirmed seeing significant numbers of them from this era in Texas. But typically, little exploration has been conducted nor documentation recorded of their age or numbers.

Hawaii is known to contain some portraits from this era and two examples can be found in the Richard Meyer Archives (p. 132). Professor Meyer also confirms he's seen portraits from this era around Seattle and other Pacific Northwest cities.

The scarcity of documented information on photo-ceramic memorial portraits underscores the need to recognize the artistic and historical relevance of this overlooked national heritage. Though gravestone enthusiasts have often noted, enjoyed and photographed some of the more interesting memorial portraits, the vast majority of photo-ceramic portraits go unappreciated, undocumented and ignored.

Near-century-old portraits continue to disappear every year. An estimated 40%-50% of all portraits from this era have already vanished or been damaged beyond recognition. There are no organized efforts to preserve or document their images.

Does the artistic and historical significance of these photo-ceramic portraits diminish because they are mounted on gravestones rather than displayed in museums? When photographed and presented as they are in the *Forgotten Faces*, few would deny their artistic merit, emotional appeal and historical relevance. If 25,000 to 35,000 intact portraits still exist, it is certain they are diminishing at a steady rate. Does this trend merit intervention?

In the four years since I began photographing memorial portraits I have witnessed scores of portraits fall from headstones, suffer irreparable damage from vandalism or simply vanish, leaving only the characteristic oval shape on the stone. Their continued disappearance represents cultural negligence. The images these portraits preserve are unique yet universal. They belong to the families. They belong to history. They deserve better.

Forgotten Faces, due to location and circumstance, preserves the images from those of predominately Catholic backgrounds. The opportunity to capture the large number of portraits from Jewish cemeteries, whose descendents also revere the art, awaits only the intent and effort of interested parties to do so. The cache of Jewish portraits from this era represents a significant number and remains a treasure yet to be discovered.

The Significance of Postmortem Photographs on Tombstones

A postmortem memorial portrait is a photograph of a person who was deceased at the time the photograph was taken. Although often viewed as morbid or macabre today, postmortem photographs were commonplace and highly valued in the 50 years before and after the 20th century. Their earlier popularity derived from the fact they often represented the last and only opportunity to possess an image of the person.[5] This made them particularly useful for documenting the final, and typically only, images of young children. To create these portraits "children could be arranged in a parent's lap, in a coffin or resting peacefully."[6] This is noted in the postmortem examples of Holy Cross, the Italian Cemetery and Richard Meyer Archives.

---

[5] Dr. Stanley B. Burns, *Death in America*

[6] Maureen Taylor, Uncovering Your Ancestry through Family Photographs (p60)

With infant mortality rates far higher than they are today, postmortem photographs provided loved ones with lasting images of children whose lives were unexpectedly cut short. "Many youngsters never lived long enough for parents to have a photograph taken." [7]

In his comprehensive and fascinating DVD, *Death in America,* Dr. Stanley B. Burns tells us that many families simply did not give their children names during the first several months of life because there was such a high probability of death before the age of one. In these cases, the children's gravestone inscription simply consisted of "Baby." One of the two Holy Cross headstones containing two postmortem portraits verifies this. One of the postmortem portraits simply bears the name of "Baby." That gravestone, surname Pombo, contains a total of three portraits. Two are postmortems and one picture is of a third child who lived only one year and four days, sadly underscoring Dr. Burns' account of the high incidence of death during the first year of life.

Some believe these photographs were a comfort to grieving family members. Jay Ruby, author of *Secure the Shadow – Death and Photography in America,* contends, as many now believe, that these photographs are "normative and even therapeutic for mourners." Postmortem photographs help mourners through bereavement. But just how rare are they?

Matt Hucke, author of *Graveyards of Chicago: The People, History, Art, and Lore of Cook* County Cemeteries has recalled seeing two, possibly more, among the hundreds of Chicago's cemeteries with thousands of memorial portraits from the early 20th century. Hucke says he has "never" witnessed a tombstone containing more than one postmortem portrait, as found in Holy Cross.

Holy Cross contains seven postmortem portraits – all of them children. Two of the stones, each containing two intact postmortem portraits, constitute a rare find, especially today. This was not always the case. Helen Sclair, Laurel Gabel and other informed sources confirm Chicago's St. Casimir cemetery may have contained more than 50 postmortems of children as recent as a few decades ago. They remember several tombstones contained more than one postmortem. But few, if any, remain today. The apparent theft of these rare artifacts – an allegedly organized and systematic removal – represents a tragic and irreparable loss.

The disappearance of postmortems in Chicago emphasizes the importance of those still remaining in Holy Cross. The Holy Cross cache, with its two stones containing two postmortems, represents an invaluable anthropological reserve of these important artifacts. Single postmortem photographs can still be found; the Italian Cemetery in Colma contains at least seven. The existence of the postmortem portrait of the Baiocchi twins denotes this collection an extremely valuable preserve of these rare artifacts. One postmortem was also found in Colma's Greek Orthodox cemetery. That constitutes a total of 15 postmortem portraits in Colma's interred population of approximately one million.

---

[7] *Sharon DeBartolo Carmack, Your Guide to Cemetery Research (p163)*

If this ratio holds true elsewhere, Chicago may be an exception with higher concentration, then postmortems on tombstones, if not rare, are valued discoveries not often encountered. Considering the fact that there are virtually no new postmortems mounted on tombstones and the older ones are decreasing in number, finding a single postmortem on every 67,000 tombstones is an uncommon experience.

Chicago's cemeteries certainly retain a significant number. The postmortem examples of Richard Meyer confirm their presence and unusual imagery. But the reported disappearance and apparent theft of these rare works of art further emphasizes the need to photograph and document them.

Modern society eschews their public display. However, they represent valued historical artifacts that mirror and preserve the culture in which they were created and revered. It is likely that only a few hundred, at most, still exist in the United States. It is important to capture and preserve these rare images from the past before it is not longer possible to do so.

In addition to its postmortem photographs, The Holy Cross collection of memorial portraits is important on several counts, but it may be most noteworthy for exposing the enormous potential of what still awaits discovery. It underscores what needs to be done and the necessity for doing it.

That remains the real significance of the Holy Cross portraits. Its large and beautiful collection of photo-ceramic portraits represents an art form missing from our culture's awareness and appreciation. By overlooking cemeteries as sources of retrievable art, we may lose irreplaceable heirlooms from our immigrant past. The importance of the Holy Cross treasure trove transcends its own inherent value. Its true significance reveals what wonders we are missing as much as those that we have.

CHAPTER FOUR

History and Technology of Early 20th Century Memorial Portraiture

In 1839, Jacques Daguerre introduced photography to the world by demonstrating his daguerreotype image on glass before the French Academy of Sciences. Less than two decades later, French photographers Bulot and Cattin were successful in fixing a photographic image to a porcelain enamel, firing it in a kiln and effectively bonding pictures on porcelain, metal, china and other surfaces. They patented the process in England in 1854.

Over the next half century, these methods were modified and refined. Today the techniques and ingredients for producing durable photographic images on porcelain remain complex. The early process combined a photographer's expertise, a chemist's proficiency, a physicist's laboratory and the patience of a saint.

Early 20th Century Process for Reproducing Photographs on a Ceramic or Metal Surface

To create a memorial portrait, friends or family of the deceased first selected a photograph. The portrait maker rephotographed the original on a large negative; greater size produces finer detail. The original photograph was retouched to isolate the subject and present the person in his or her most becoming appearance. The refurbished photo was photographed again. That negative was reproduced on a glass plate coated with a colloidal film of silver nitrate and other chemicals. Then the plate was washed with water and fixed with potassium cyanide. The colloidal film was removed from the plate and washed repeatedly. The exact chemical combinations varied, each photographer using chlorides or nitrates of gold, silver, platinum and its elemental cousins, palladium and iridium. These stable metals vigorously resist degeneration from heat, sunlight and other chemicals.

At this stage, the photographic image was composed of durable metals. Still colloidal in form, the delicate image was placed on a ceramic surface and fired in a kiln. Intense heat destroyed the colloidal, leaving the image intact on the ceramic. Then the ceramic, coated with a hard, dense resin, was fired in a kiln five to six times. The repeated application of heat hardened the components into an impenetrable mass.

The intense temperatures bonded the final image to the ceramic surface. Then it was coated with tough, transparent resin. According to the Society of Dutch Enamellers' publication *The Art of Glass on Metal,* the resulting image was composed of "immutable" metals encased in an "impermeable substance." Memorial portraits manufactured in this manner can survive outdoors for hundreds of years.

This process, the specific metals and chemicals, varied significantly. The precise recipes were guarded by their creators in the same way corporations conceal their proprietary technical secrets today. The craftsmen passed their formulas on to a select few. Manufacturers of memorial portraits today still cloak their techniques in secrecy.

Many Modern Products Possess Inferior Quality and Less Durability

The early ingredients and procedures used to create memorial portraits at the turn of the century are still costly to duplicate today. More economical components and lowered durability standards have forced some manufacturers to produce portraits that degenerate in less than half a century.

The funeral industry's unwritten "forty-year rule" declares that most grave sites go unattended after 40 years. With this in mind, many of today's products are not made to equal the longevity of those created in the early 1900s, though several modern manufacturers do produce memorial portraits capable of lasting for centuries, most notably J.A. Dedouch, Paradise Pictures and PermaFrame Inc.

Memorial Portraiture: 1900 to Modern Times

Though patented by the French, it was the Italians who popularized portraits on tombstones. During the first decades of the 1900s, their use flourished throughout Eastern and Southern Europe. When these immigrants arrived in the United States, they perpetuated the tradition wherever they settled. From New York to Chicago, Georgia to Texas and the shores of the Pacific, memorial portraits from this era still remain intact. Though continually disappearing, many cemeteries still shelter these relics.

The majority of portraits found on headstones in Holy Cross Cemetery were produced in Europe. However, a U.S. manufacturer from that era is still an industry leader today. In 1893, J.A. Dedouch of Chicago produced the first American-made memorial portraits. The Dedouch family passed on their techniques from generation to generation. Richard Stannard, grandson of J.A. Dedouch, has managed the company for the last decade. Dedouch produces from 12,000 to 15,000 memorial portraits a year, contributing more than a million memorial portraits in the last century. The company's products, called Dedos in the industry, are still produced in much the same way as they were at the turn of the century.

European designs often display a characteristic circle of gold around the image; Dedos do not unless specifically requested. Manufactured on copper plates rather than solid ceramics, Dedouch portraits populate many of the oldest cemeteries across our nation. Sometimes called the "Coca-Cola of Memorial Portraits," Dedouch defines the standard of longevity for United States manufacturers, though their story has recently undergone a dramatic change.

Oak Park Ceramics in Hillsdale, Illinois, splintered off from Dedouch in 1946. It utilizes similar procedures in its manufacturing process and remains a regarded vendor of the art.

West Coast manufacturer Paradise Pictures, located in Paradise, California, also produces memorial portraits designed for maximum durability utilizing the highest-quality components. The owners of Paradise Pictures, Michael Sandquist and David Hopper, afford a level of expertise and technical acumen regarding this esoteric art that belies their 1991 inception. According to *www.ParadisePictures.com*, Paradise "uses ancient processes for firing the inorganic pigments/oxides into a glass matrix, just as it was done over 145 years ago in the first monument portraits."

This technique allows Paradise to offer comprehensive replacement guarantees for the lifetime of their product at no charge. This guarantee includes unlikely image fading and even portraits that may be vandalized or broken by cemetery machinery.

Permaframe Inc., in Boca Rotan, Florida, also offers a lifetime guarantee with their porcelain-based products. They also offer design variations that include a metal frame and hinged door to further protect the image of the deceased. Both Permaframe and Paradise offer comprehensive guarantees that assure you your memorial portrait will last well beyond the boundaries of the "forty-year rule."

Italy's Rossato Giovanni, a well-known European manufacturer, has produced superior ceramic memorial portraits for generations and maintains a significant U.S. market penetration. Photokeramik of Austria and Willems Classics of the Netherlands are additional European sources for memorial portraits.

The Internet Era Begins

The Internet has changed the way the world does business and memorial portraits are no exception. When I first interviewed Richard Stannard of Dedouch, I was surprised that Dedouch had no Website and the company offered no e-mail contact. Therefore, I was not surprised to hear that three brothers from Canada, Guy, Paul and Pierre d'Anjou, have purchased America's oldest memorial portrait manufacturer, J.A. Dedouch. The Quebec-based PSM – Picture Specialists for Memorials-acquired Dedouch in early 2004. This marks the end of an era for memorial portraiture. Dedouch's century – old name, like Xerox or Kleenex, was synonymous with the product itself.

The Internet has, as for many businesses, influenced the way memorial portraits are sold. Though many still rely on the cemetery or funeral director to acquire their memorial portrait, more people purchase theirs from companies doing business on the Internet.

Paradise Pictures in California and PermaFrame in Florida both transcend their state boundaries and do significant business over the Internet as well as directly with cemeteries. The Internet allows for direct contact with the manufacturer and increases the customer's access to information, choices and procedures for acquiring exactly the product they want.

The tightly guarded methodology for manufacturing durable memorial portraits remains highly specialized. It requires customized training that is hard to acquire outside the tight-knit industry. These resources will rarely be the least expensive option for a memorial. Longevity costs slightly more – its value to you and your loved ones, apparent only centuries from now. You may want to request the guarantee in writing if you have any questions about how long the product will last.

Today, memorial portraits come in a variety of sizes, black and white or color and quality products with a comprehensive guarantee cost approximately $300 for a typical 2-inch by 3-inch oval portrait. Larger portraits cost proportionately more. If you want the product to outlast the 40-year rule, do business with companies that offer full guarantees.

A final note, literally, if you want to have a memorial portrait on your own headstone. You may want to select your own photo now and designate it as such in your will or with family members. You may even want to have it made before the need arises. It is a luxury most of those featured in this book did not have and it affords a certain level of satisfaction to know how you will appear to those who know you only by the picture they may be observing a century or more from now.

What is the difference between an epitaph and an inscription?

"Epitaph, in its strictest (and oldest) sense refers to rhymed verse (of the type popular, for instance on 18th and 19th century gravestones), though more recently it is often extended to be a descriptor of any unrhymed personal expression (e.g., "He was loved by all"). Many stones, of course, have no true epitaphs at all, only other inscriptional data providing names, dates, perhaps place of birth."

- Professor Richard E. Meyer is the co-author of *The Revival Styles in American Memorial Art*

Photo-Gallery II

The Children's Perpetual Care Section of Holy Cross Cemetery

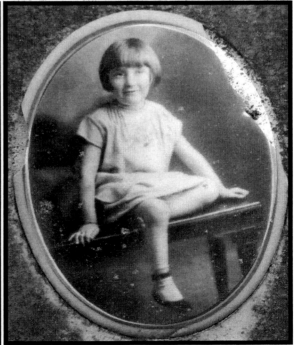

Fred Hugli Jr.
1917—1920
Frank's large round eyes speak to us.

Gillette Labro
Died in 1927 - age 5 years 6 months.
Gillette sits casually on one leg.

Lillian Ailand
December 17, 1917 to July 8, 1919

Tony Dragovan
died Dec. 22, 1923, Age 2

The Significance of the First Holy Communion Attire

Children dressed to receive their First Holy Communion is a common theme in memorial portraits from Catholic cemeteries and throughout *Forgotten Faces*. Pages 70 and 76 group examples of girls and boys but other illustrations can be seen throughout the book. A child's First Holy Communion was often his or her first occasion to be formally photographed. It represents a major milestone in a Catholic's religious journey – their first time in communion with Christ through reception of the sacrament of the Holy Eucharist and coming into full communion with the mother Church.

For this blessed occasion, the children donned attire rich in symbolic meaning. Girls dressed entirely in white, often with a veil, symbolic of purity of Spirit. Boys wore a white ribbon on their arms to signify their similar status. Many posed with calla lilies to reinforce this theme. Most hold their missals and their rosaries wrapped around their hands. So attired, they represent the embodiment man free from sin and ready to receive the pure Spirit of Christ.

Teresa Ronco

Born in San Francisco 1904, died in San Francisco 1919
Teresa wears her school uniform and holds a
diploma between her forefingers.

Girls wear the White Veil of Purity for their First Holy Communion

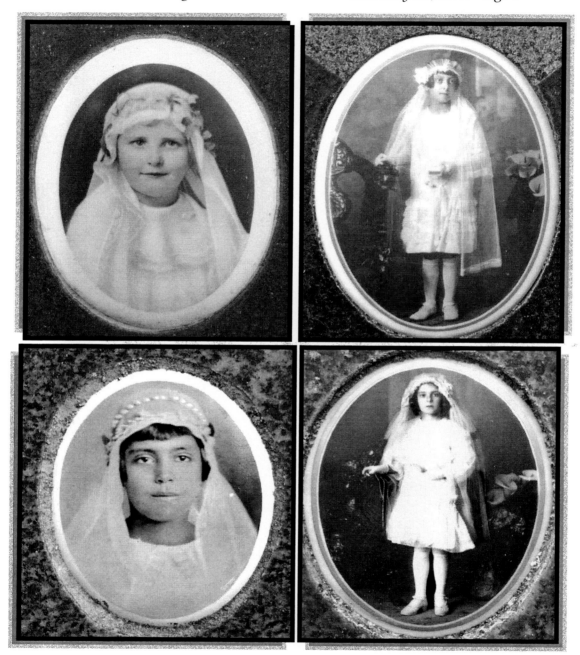

Mary R. Murphy
1928—1940 Age 12

Rose Lombardi
died May 29, 1929 Age 9

Irma Valladeras
1923—1931 Age 8

Angeles Ardanaz
1913—1922 Age 9

Alice Portos
November 20, 1911 to March 17, 1921
Alice, whose feet do not touch the floor, holds a pull-string purse and a doll
whose head rests on a teddy bear's head. The bear's feet poke out under
Alice's arm. Note the size of the bow in Alice's hair.

*Rose, with her two bows, stares straight
into the camera and into our eyes.*

Ana Ybarra
December 2, 1911 to April 18, 1922
Ana's stone lies in a secluded area, her portrait almost hidden from sight.

Emilie Sautier
Died 1916
Age 2 years 8 months

John Jelencich   *Died 1917, Age 2*
John sits on a hand-stitched quilt in his high-chair with a toy animal and a smile.

Carmen Rodriguez
1899—1910   Age 11

Andres J. Lezamis
1918—1925   Age 7

The headstone of
Carmen Rodriguez

Alice A. Clarke
Died May 17, 1921   Age 9

Emily Elise Cousette

1914—1921

Emily's portrait shows her eyes cast downward, producing mood and
perspective on the subject. She was 7 years old when she died.

Boys dressed for their First Holy Communion

display their missals, rosaries and white ribbons of purity.

Bernard Pressans — Died 1924 age 13

Joseph E. Murphy — 1907 1923

James Curtin — 1910 - 1923

IN LOVING MEMORY OF
JOSEPH E. MURPHY
1907-1923
FATHER
CORNELIUS MURPHY
DIED APR. 12, 1926
MOTHER
ELIZABETH 1950
SULLIVAN
MURPHY

Rodolpho and Anita Lopez

Rodolpho A. Lopez
1918 — 1924
(Left)
Anita A. Lopez
1927 — 1931
(Below)

The Lopez's stone lies in the children's section of Holy Cross where the headstones, like their namesakes, are only 12 to 18 inches tall and one must bend very low to the ground to see the many portraits of children in this section devoted specifically to them.

Rodolpho seems to genuinely enjoy wearing his clown suit. Anita, with short hair and locket, assumes a more serious pose. The children lived without ever seeing each other.

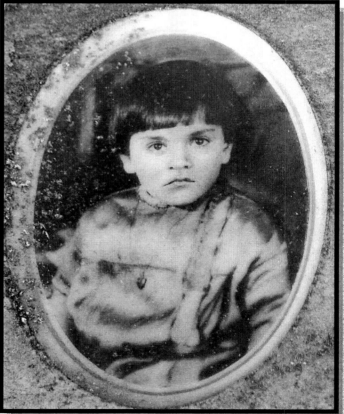

Myrna M. Lee *1934—1935*
Myrna is one of three portrait subjects with Chinese ancestry.

Clement Oliveira *1920—1924*
Clement wears a "U.S. Navy" cap and uniform.

Rosaria Reta ▶

December 18, 1932
January 26, 1837

The children's section contains many monuments with protective angels atop gravestones.

Rosario's angel (right) provides a good example of the popular stone.

She smiles looking to her left while resting both hands on a covered bench.

Donald Adanza   1930—1941 Age 9

Donald's stone lies flat on the ground. Although the majority of portraits are mounted on vertical head stones Holy Cross has several sections that contain portraits from this era mounted flat. Many cemeteries have policies outlawing vertical headstones making those sections much easier to maintain.

Henriette Cazajous
January 10, 1907 -
November 19, 1921

Henriette's portrait is accompanied by her father Jules who died three years after her at age 45. Her mother, Justine, lived until the age of 95 and died in 1980.

Postmortem Portraits of Holy Cross

Holy Cross harbors a cluster of seven postmortem portraits. Two of the headstones display two postmortems each. Today a single stone displaying two intact postmortems is considered rare. Two such gravestones in close proximity represent a valuable anthropological reserve of these artifacts.

The Three Angels

The Pombo interment includes three angel statues accompanying three portraits of children—two of them postmortems. Theresa Pombo (center) was born on March 9, 1938 and died on March 11, 1939. Her sisters each survived less than two weeks. Their postmortem photographs preserve their memory. Nearby the headstones of Mary Bugeja and "Two Helen" Mordus also display postmortems. The two Pombo postmortem portraits are detailed on the next page.

The Pombo stone, one of two stones displaying two postmortems each

"Baby," August 5, 1924 to August 15, 1924, and Maria Pombo, Sept. 8, 1936 to Sept. 12, 1936. The author has not determined which is Maria and which is "Baby." Theresa, March 9, 1938 to March 11, 1939 is pictured in the center of the stone. Death rates for children under 12 were so high during this era that parents often did not name their children until age one and hence only "baby" was used on the tombstone.

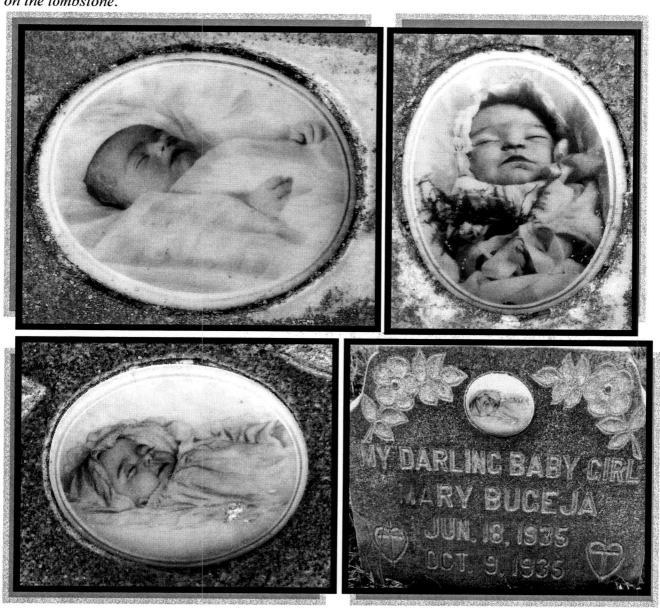

Mary Bugeja

Mary Bugeja lived from June 18, 1935 to October 9, 1935. She represents the fifth postmortem portrait clustered in the section of Holy Cross dedicated to young children. Infants and babies were often photographed postmortem to preserve a singular, lasting image of their existence.

The Mordus Headstone

The Mordus epitaph evokes an element of mystery. The inscription indicates that both girls were named Helen, but according to cemetery records, "Helen" died on Feb. 21, 1914, and "Ellen" on October 22, 1923.

It is possible that the record does not reflect the family's actual preference and they named their second child after the first, as the epitaph implies. Dr. Stanley B. Burns, author of <u>Death in America</u>, tells us this was common practice during this era.

Archival research shows that the first Helen was originally buried in a different section of Holy Cross and moved to this location in 1940.

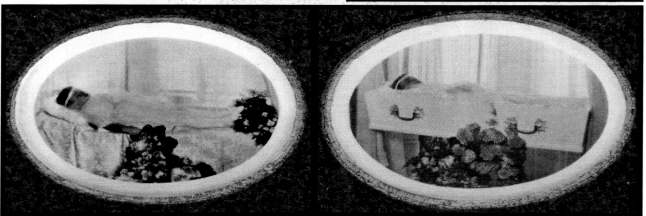

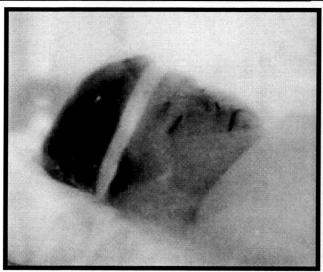
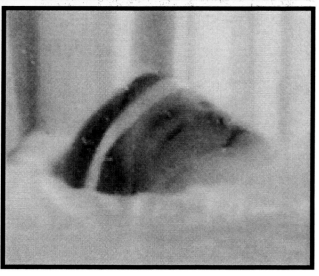

The mystery of the Mordus epitaph deepens, as close-ups of "Two Helen" reveals a remarkable likeness between the two girls. Their surroundings and close-ups are so similar that it looks as if the two photographs were taken at the same place and time. Do these images appear to be two different girls born nine years apart? You decide.

CHAPTER FIVE

Memorial Portraiture Across Cultures

By Lisa Montanarelli

Photographic tombstones never became as widespread in this country as in Southern and Eastern Europe and in Latin America. In the United States, they are most common among immigrant groups, especially among Italian Americans and Jews from Eastern Europe, who brought this custom from their homelands. In California, they are also common among Latino populations.

Holy Cross displays an unusually diverse array of portraits, representing immigrants from at least 28 nations. Many of these people came from cultures that viewed life and death much differently from mainstream "Americanized" society. While we can only speculate on the intentions of individuals who chose these memorials, we can say something about the cultures that favor photographic tombstones. In this essay, I consider these memorials in the context of Italian American, Jewish and Latin American culture—their mourning customs and their views of life and death.

Many North Americans have never heard of photographic tombstones. This is perhaps due to the denial of death in 20th-century American culture. As Jay Ruby writes in *Securing the Shadow*:

> Attitudes toward death in American society have had a complex history. In the nineteenth century it was a common topic of polite discussion. Mourning was a normal part of the pubic life of most adults. Widowhood was a primary, lifelong social role for many women. And then it all changed. From the beginning of the twentieth century until the 1970s, death became a forbidden subject among the "Americanized" middle class. The slightest sign of distress at the death of a family member was regarded as pathological. (7)

This denial of death was a privilege due to declining death rates in 20th-century America. For most of history people weren't able to deny death. It was all around them. This is still true in many parts of the world and in some U.S. populations. In the early 20th century, many immigrants lived in poverty and had higher mortality rates than the average U.S. citizen. Many came from famished regions of the world, where death was a more frequent companion. When these immigrants came to the United States, they often found that their customs conflicted with mainstream American culture, which frowned on sentimental displays of grief and attachment to the deceased. Nonetheless, many ethnic groups held on to the mourning and memorializing customs of their homelands as a way to maintain their cultural identity. The portraits in *Forgotten Faces* were made at a time when American society frowned upon overt displays of mourning. In this sense, they testify to immigrants' success at keeping their cultural traditions alive.

Photographic tombstones are perhaps most popular among cultures that have an ongoing relationship to the dead—either in the literal sense of communicating with dead relatives or in the more figurative sense of preserving cultural identity. In the United States, these memorials are generally considered most common among Italian Americans. John Matturi is one of the few scholars to write on a specific culture's relation to photographic tombstones. His essay "Windows in the Garden: Italian-American Memorialization and the American Cemetery" considers how photographic tombstones conflicted with the dominant North American cemetery tradition.

In the January 1929 issue of the trade journal *Park and Cemetery*, landscape architect Ray F. Wyrick contrasts the cemeteries of Havana, Italy and France with those of North America: "Their ideal seems to be to try to keep grief alive for a long time, and we try to soften grief and think of the graves of our dead as melted into the peace of a quiet landscape" (Wyrick 306, cited in Matturi 14).

According to Matturi, the cemeteries of Havana, France and Italy "serve not so much to 'keep grief alive,' as Wyrick assumes, but to keep the relationship between the living and the dead alive" (18). Havana, France and Italy have large Catholic populations. Their memorial practices reflect the Catholic doctrine that the living have an obligation to pray for dead loved ones in order to speed their passage through purgatory, a transitional state in which souls who die in sin are purified. Matturi observes:

Within Catholic religious culture, particularly that of Mediterranean countries, the realm of the spirit is not utterly transcendent to the world, and social and familial relationships and obligations do not end with death. To ignore or forget one's dead is to violate basic norms and expectations. (16)

A monument that keeps the dead alive in memory would help mourners fulfill their obligations.

If a survivor has a responsibility to maintain a continued relationship with a dead relative, the most appropriate cemetery monument will be one that can best serve to elicit a vivid memory of the deceased… The photograph thus serves as a kind of window of imagination through which one can maintain a relationship with a deceased family member. (Matturi 23-5)

Joseph J. Inguanti notes that many Italian immigrants also adorned the walls of their homes with oval-shaped photographs of deceased relatives and prayed to the dead as one would pray to a favorite saint. As I mentioned in the introduction, a grave marker is both a personal observation of grief and a public memorial. According to Inguanti, "the photoceramic portrait establishes the important link between the private space of the Italian-American home and the public space of the cemetery" (16-7). In many cases, the memorial portrait was made from a copy of a photograph that hung in the family's home. The portrait on the tombstone also served the same purpose as the photo in the home. Both reminded the family of their duties to the dead.

Matturi describes some of the rituals that surrounded photo-ceramic tombstones:

Italian-Americans… have continued to maintain the cemetery as an active site of ritualized communion with the dead at a time when the American cemetery has been seen by many to have become a purely functional site of interment…. Weekend visits to the plots of family members are frequent, and plants, flowers, and other ornaments are routinely placed on the grave and often maintained for decades after a death… elderly family members will be seen standing before the grave engaged in deep and serious conversation with a dead spouse, parent or child. In other cases, holiday greeting cards will be placed on the grave with personal inscriptions of love and continued emotional affiliation. (18)

Though Matturi focuses on Italian Americans, Latin Americans also have rituals of communing with dead family members at their gravesites. For instance, on November 1 and 2, the Catholic All Saints' Day and All Souls' Day, Mexicans and many other Latin Americans celebrate the Days of the Dead (*Dias de Todos Muertos*), when the deceased return to visit their living loved ones. People leave food at the graves of departed relatives. "Their spirits are expected to come out and eat the food… Often there is a big picnic in the cemetery… The family, which includes both the living and the dead, dines and communes together" (Younoszai 75-6).

Many Latin Americans who come to the U.S. continue to celebrate the Days of the Dead. Some of the immigrants pictured in these pages came from Chile, Ecuador, Guatemala, Honduras, Mexico, Nicaragua and Peru. They probably observed this holiday.

It is also worth noting that the rituals surrounding the Days of the Dead are not specifically Catholic. These customs combine official Catholic holydays, pre-Spanish Aztec rituals and medieval Spanish folk customs. Similarly the way any culture or immigrant group views life and death often involves intersections and amalgamations of many cultures. Although Holy Cross is a Catholic cemetery, many of the immigrants shown in the portraits may have practiced a blend of Catholicism and local customs from their homelands. Every nation, including the United States, contains numerous small-scale societies with populations of fewer than one million and typically fewer than 100,000 (Rosenblatt 28-9). Small-scale societies tend to view death and life quite differently from the dominant Euro-American culture. Many, if not most of these groups, believe in an ongoing relationship between the living and the dead.

While photo tombstones are most popular among Italian Americans, they are also common among Jews who trace their ancestry to Eastern Europe. Mount Zion Cemetery in Maspeth, Queens houses hundreds of photographic tombstones. Ruby notes that the Jewish cemeteries within Chicago's Oak Woods Cemetery contain numerous photo tombstones as well. In a study of Jewish cemeteries, anthropologist David Gradwohl found that these monuments were more common in Conservative and Orthodox cemeteries than in Reform cemeteries. Gradwohl suspects that this difference is due to the ancestry of the people who bury their dead in these places. Photo-ceramic grave markers are more common among Eastern European Jews as well as Christians (244). The Slavonic section of Holy Cross Cemetery contains an especially dense cluster of portraits. Ruby adds, "photographs can be found on Jewish tombstones in Russia, Poland, all of the Baltic republics, and Israel" (198n12).

The prevalence of photo tombstones in Jewish cemeteries may come as a surprise to some, "given a general prohibition against graven images, designed in part to prevent the worship of ancestors" (Ruby 172). In the Catholic cultures of southern Italy and Latin America, it is not uncommon to pray to the image of a saint or even a dead relative, and memorial portraits sometimes served this purpose. Judaism, on the other hand, forbids the use of images in worship. It thus seems that photo tombstones must play a different role in Jewish culture.

The large number of Jewish photo tombstones no doubt reflects the widespread use of these memorials in Eastern Europe. Perhaps it also reflects the importance of honoring the dead. As Ellen Levine writes in "Jewish Views and Customs on Death," "two of the most important commandments in Judaism are to honor the dead and comfort the mourner" (98).

Judaism has perhaps the most elaborate mourning rituals of any culture. In the Jewish ritual calendar, the community joins in common remembrance of the dead five times per year. In the case of mourning a close relative, "Jewish tradition demands... a concrete timetable of mourning.... a set of stages that regulate a return from the abyss of grief" (Heilman 120). These stages include Shivah, the seven days following burial, Shloshim, the thirty days following burial, in which Kaddish, the prayer most associated with mourning is recited daily, Yud-beit chodesh, the twelve months following burial, and the Yahrzeit, when the family gathers on the anniversary of the death. In *When a Jew Dies*, Samuel C. Heilman observes:

> Many of the... mourning rituals are an effort to compensate for the swift funeral and burial and to help rearrange the relationship between the dead and the living.... These days mark a gradual coming to terms with the undeniable reality of death, the development of a new kind of relationship both to the deceased and to the community, and ultimately an altered identity for the mourner and the dead. (120)

Shivah is an example of a mourning ritual that helps the living come to terms with a death in the family. During Shivah, the seven days following burial, mourners are forbidden to work. They wear rent clothing and sit on low stools, while receiving guests in their home. These observances make it impossible to forget the reality of death, but also help family come to terms with this reality.

Some traditional Jews understand their relation to the dead quite literally. According to Heilman, "there is a mystical (some might say imagined) belief among traditional Jews that, particularly in the first days following the funeral, the spirit of the one who has died is unwilling immediately to leave its bodily form" (119). Some believe that the soul of the deceased hovers near the body and observes the funeral.

The relationship between the living and the dead does not have to be taken literally. Even those who do not believe in an afterlife can have a relation to the dead in the sense of history or cultural identity. Heilman writes: "As long as we are connected to those who have gone before us, we are not dead, not as a people and not as individuals. As long as there are those who recall our lives, we live" (234).

Perhaps more than any other factor, the presence of photo tombstones in Jewish cemeteries reflects a strong sense of cultural heritage and a belief that the dead have relevance to our present lives. Our cultural identity depends on maintaining a connection to the dead—a relationship to past and future generations. As historian Charles O. Jackson writes:

> denying the dead world a role in the living world... is after all a rejection of both our past and future. If the dead are simply gone and irrelevant as those presently alive are soon to be, the chain of historical continuity is broken at every link. (54)

Italian American, Latin American and Jewish cultures share customs that keep the dead alive —either literally, in the sense of communicating with the dead, or figuratively, in the sense of preserving the dead in memory. By keeping the dead alive in memory these cultures keep their heritage alive as well. This is perhaps why photo tombstones are most popular among immigrant groups with a strong sense of cultural identity. If the dead simply cease to exist, we lose our own history, our background, and our roots.

Works Cited

Dethlefson, Edwin S. 1981. The Cemetery and Culture Change: Archaeological Focus and Ethnographic Practice. *In Modern Material Culture: The Archaeology of Us.* Edited by Richard A. Gould and Michael B. Schiffer. New York: Academic Press, 137-160.

Gradwohl, David Mayer and Hanna Rosenberg. 1988. This is the Pillar of Rachel's Grave unto This Day: Cemeteries in Lincoln, Nebraska. In *Persistence and Flexibility: Anthropological Perspectives on the American Jewish Experience.* Edited by Walter P. Zenner. Albany: SUNY Press, 223-259.

Green, Judith Strupp. 1980. The Days of the Dead in Oaxaca, Mexico: An Historical Inquiry. In *Death and Dying: Views from Many Cultures.* Edited by Richard A. Kalish. Baywood Publishing, 56-71.

Heilman, Samuel C. 2001. *When a Jew Dies.* Berkeley: University of California Press.

Inguanti, Joseph J. 2000. Domesticating the Grave: Italian-American Memorial Practices at New York's Calvary Cemetery. In *Markers XVII.* Edited by Richard E. Meyer. Greenfield, Massachusetts: Association for Gravestone Studies.

Jackson, Charles O. 1980. Death Shall Have No Dominion: The Passing of the World of the Dead in America. In *Death and Dying: Views from Many Cultures.* Edited by Richard A. Kalish. Baywood Publishing, 47-55.

Jackson, Kenneth and Camilo José Vergara. 1989. *Silent Cities*. New York: Princeton Architectural Press.

Levine, Ellen. 1997. Jewish views and customs on death. In *Death and Bereavement Across Cultures*. Edited by Colin Murray Parkes, Pittu Laungani and Bill Young. New York: Brunner-Routledge, 98-130.

Matturi, John. 1993. Windows in the Garden: Italian-American Memorialization and the American Cemetery. In *Ethnicity and the American Cemetery*. Edited by Richard E. Meyer. Bowling Green, Ohio: Bowling Green State University Popular Press, 14-35.

Rosenblatt, Paul C. 1997. Grief in Small-Scale Societies. In *Death and Bereavement Across Cultures*. Edited by Colin Murray Parkes, Pittu Laungani and Bill Young. New York: Brunner-Routledge, 27-51.

Ruby, Jay. 1995. *Secure the Shadow: Death and Photography in America*. Cambridge and London: MIT Press.

Snyder, Daniel Gyger. 1971. American Family Memorial Imagery, the Photograph and the Search for Immortality. Unpublished M.A. thesis. Albuquerque: University of New Mexico.

Wyrick, Ray F. 1929. Cemetery Travelogues: VIII. Havana. *Park and Cemetery* 38 (January).

Younoszai, Barbara. 1993. Mexican American Perspectives Related to Death. In *Ethnic Variations in Dying, Death and Grief*. Edited by Donald P. Irish, Kathleen F. Lundquist, and Vivian Jenkins Nelsen. Washington, D.C.: Taylor & Francis, 67-78.

CHAPTER SIX

Windows in Time: The Unique Characteristics of Memorial Portraits

Memorial portraits differ from other photographs. Intended to celebrate life's milestones, they instead convey its mortality. They fuse popular and funerary art into a singular expression of lasting individuality.

When you view the portraits of the well-attired Fourgous family (p. 47) you feel the echoes of another era. Memorial portraits act as time capsules, revealing intimate moments from a life concluded. They connect us with a history personal yet universal. Through their faces, we travel in time and sense the life of another, inaccessible yet substantial.

Life connected to death

The art of memorial portraiture establishes relationship through imagery. We find ourselves standing with one foot in life, the other in death. This stance evokes emotion.

Memorial portraiture builds a bridge, but bars its crossing. Mutuality is established, then broken. This is another characteristic of memorial portraiture that makes it different from other photographs. We encounter a vibrant, smiling face only to realize it represents the conclusion of that life; it conveys the deceased's final statement.

Dorothy Kristulovich's portrait (p. 50) illustrates this dissonance. She is wearing her wedding gown, festooned with flowers and lace. Her epitaph hints at how much more of her story there is. The stone inscription typically relates the date of her death, April 20, 1929, then adds: "Joseph Kristulovich Born & Died April 20, 1929." Twenty-eight-year-old Dorothy died giving birth to her son Joseph. He is buried with her. Her husband, Tony, born the same year as Dorothy, lived to age 60 and passed away in 1961. Thirty-two years after losing his wife and son, he was laid to rest with his family again.

Dorothy's portrait marries her picture with her epitaph. Her story emerges, providing us with a depiction of her life and her death. Dorothy demonstrates this attribute of memorial portraiture. It creates a relationship that can never be realized. It makes us want to know more about the person in the picture. Then it places that person beyond our reach. It makes us ambivalent, delighted and sad at the same time.

The Dual Nature of Memorial Portraits

Memorial portraits possess another duality. They communicate a mixed message because the photos were never meant to be memorials. The picture of Alice Clark (p. 74) commemorates her first Holy Communion. It reveals Alice, encouraged by the photographer, tilting her head and peering straight into the camera. It provides a sense of the moment, a feeling of immediacy. Alice is involved in the present. Looking at her, we are too. That is the goal of photographic portraiture. That is how it is meant to work.

But Alice's photograph, which celebrates a joyous milestone in her life, was never intended to represent her in death. Memorial portraits reframe the moment and the person. Rather than signifying festivity, it now represents the end of Alice's life. Memorial portraits create this contradiction. This can be confusing for the observer.

Portraits of children magnify this emotional discord. Their youthful innocence defies the stark reality of their death, a juxtaposition of opposites that reflects the dual nature of memorial portraits. They evoke a quality seldom encountered elsewhere. Photographs commemorating joyous events express, instead, an unintended finality that cannot be dismissed.

Memorial Portraits Tell a Personal Story

Photographs used as memorial portraits were often selected to tell a particular story about their subject. The subjects rarely choose their own picture. Their selection encourages insights about the deceased and often details of the era in which they lived.

The portrait of Annie Corcoran (p. 39) is an example. Annie wears a brooch containing the visible portrait of another person. Absent loved ones were often included in photographs to represent their presence in the subject's life.[8]

So it is with many of these portraits. Whether we see Anthony Mello (p. 35) in his fireman's garb or Mary O'Neill (p. 171) in her nurse's uniform, their portraits provide insights into their private lives, telling the story their loved ones wanted told, selecting a photograph intended to convey their message.

Inscriptions on headstones define boundaries of life: Margrete O'Neill, December 12, 1904, to September 22, 1925. Portraits bestow a human face upon those borders in time. Portraits articulate the dialect of imagery and symbol. We know the face through the power of its own expression. Neither time nor death extinguishes its humanity. Memorial portraits perpetuate life. That is their intent, their nature and their value. That is the story they have to tell. That is what makes them different. Their message stands apart and stands alone.

[8] Maureen Taylor *Uncovering Your Ancestry through Family Photographs* (p60)

- Examples of the Art Form -
From the United States
and Europe.

Photo-ceramic memorial portraits originated in Europe and populated the United States through the immigrants who settled here. The following pages depict examples of this funerary art form from those who have developed and advanced it.

The photographs presented in the Italian Cemetery in Photo-Gallery II and those of Richard Meyer and Cathy Ward in Photo-Gallery III underscore both the artistic merit and historical relevance of memorial portraiture. The photo above was taken by Constance Clare and shows portraits from Italy embedded in an engaging monument – typical of the Italians who have fostered and revered the art from its inception.

The Italian Cemetery of Colma, California

Colma's Italian cemetery, founded in 1898, contains over 50,000 interments on only 40 acres. Though less than one tenth the size of Holy Cross, the Italian Cemetery yields an extremely high concentration of early 20th-century ceramic memorial portraits. It includes more than 800 images of immigrants and first generation Italian Americans as well as Spanish Americans and Latinos.

Small, gated and located in a highly visible area, the Italian cemetery has a lower rate of vandalism than the other cemeteries in Colma. Many family vaults stand above ground and close together, making the cemetery appear as a vast marble, granite and cement walkway full of monuments and funerary art.

The Italians have refined memorial portraiture for over a century. Their tombstones display elaborate arrangements of portraits, often representing several generations of family members. Many of the photographs include sumptuous imagery, studio backgrounds and other historically significant details.

This small selection showcases the beauty of memorial portraiture, refined by the Italians who popularized this art form. The portraits honor the dead and reflect the culture's deep reverence for its ancestry.

Photo-Gallery III — The Italian Cemetery of Colma

Lillian S. Corso
March 10, 1905 to February 24, 1923, Age 17
Born in San Francisco, Lillian assumes a classic portrait pose that brings drama to a still picture. Her face in profile, Lillian gazes downward and away from the camera and us creating a sense of distant introspection.

This composite shows three women of the **Baptista Family** in one portrait. Portraits often combined separate photos that show the family together.

Caterina Viscusso was 23 when she passed away in 1921. She is pictured here in her wedding dress holding a bouquet.

Pierina Icardi *died in 1925 at the age of 31. She is joined in this portrait by her son* ***Frank*** *who was 10 months old.*

Giovanni Mordinoia was only 23 when he died in 1922. Giovanni's portrait implies an educated young man of means.

Marina Petri was 26 when she died in 1925. She is posed with a studio prop replicating a personal, home-like environment.

Rosalia and Antone Cancilla pose in casual attire with an old house, possibly theirs, in the background. Antone died in 1919 at 84 years of age. Rosalia was 83 when she passed away three years later.

This portrait tells everything about its subject that her loved ones wanted us to know. Her gravestone contains only this portrait and no inscription or epitaph of any kind. It is appropriately and uncommonly large, over ten inches in height compared to the average four inches for most portraits. Its imagery tells the subjects story. Research reveals that her name is Angelina Mazza, born on March 14, 1869 and died on January 5, 1960, age 90. The portrait above was taken sometime in the 1920's.

I Bambini

Maria Zalunardo
was 7 when she died in 1919. She is seated wearing a locket around her neck and ribbons in her hair. She holds a purse in her left hand.

Ezio Celsi
holds a toy dog and wears pantaloons wider than his shoulders. He was 3 when he died in 1923.

Frank Marciano
was born in San Francisco on September 21, 1904. He died on his birthday in 1909 at age 4.

Alfredo Bonugli
Born in Gallicano, Italy on April 3, 1918 died in San Francisco on February 26, 1922.

Civil War Veteran

Giussepe Garbone wears a civil war uniform with a GAR - Grand Army of the Republic - insignia on his hat (upper left inset) and veteran's medal (upper right inset) on his lapel. Born in 1847, he would have been 16 during the middle of the war in 1863. He died at age 74 in 1921. Proud of his service, Giussepe donned the uniform of his youth again in his latter years, perhaps at a GAR reunion, where he exhibited full honors.

Lino Costello was born in 1876 and died in 1924 at age 48. He wears a cadet's uniform

Pietro Campilongo wears the uniform of a Carabiniere – the Italian Military Police. Born in 1857, he was 59 when he died in 1916.

Amerigo Deferrari, pictured here in a World War 1 uniform, died just after the war in 1919 when still in his twenties.

Daniel Laverne was only 25 when he died in 1941. Through his portrait we understand his talents and how he wanted to be remembered.

Brothers

Olivio Rustici was born in San Francisco in 1893 and died in June, 1909.
His brother Aldino (left) was born in 1894 and died in October of 1909.
Their attire suggests a family of means.

Mother and Son

Gaetana Campisa *died in 1907 at age 56.*
Her son **Frank Arena** *died in 1944 at age 54. He is pictured here uniformed at a younger age.*

Ginao Stradi
Died November 5, 1912 at age 22
Ginao assumes a studied pose on a studio chair.

Margo Anuno
Died March 28, 1921 at age 7
Margo tilts her head in an inquisitive pose.

Aladino Guisti   1906—1920
*Aladino's hands and lower body reveal extensive
photo reconstruction.*

Pietro and Lola Barsotti
Pietro 1885—1914   Lola 1916—1918
Dates reveal Lola is not Pietro's daughter.

Anita Amanini

Born August 29, 1903, died in San Francisco October 19, 1918, Anita was 15.
Anita's portrait reveals the porcelain structure to contain fine cracks throughout its surface, giving it an appearance of age and elegance. Both complement the picture as Anita demonstrates a lot of the latter with so little of the former.

Enrico De Maria
May 5, 1919 — March 20, 1920
Enrico's focused gaze belies his youthful age.

Emelio Baldocchi
August 26, 1884 — June 31, 1902
His portrait bears the photographer's signature.

Hildalisa Hurtado *died in 1935 at age 41.*
She is buried with her sister Susie Udall who
died in 1945 at age 45.

Tomasa Garcia
age 24 in 1921 is buried with
Mildrid Perez, *1927 — 1929.*

Caterina Antonini died at age 42 in 1936. Her husband *Paul* died 36 years later in 1972 at age 88.

Mariano Alioto, born in Sicily, died at the age of 23 in 1914. His wife, *Josephina* died in 1945 at age 72.

Guiseppe Picinnin, looking dapper in his hat, died at age 43 in 1925. He is buried with his brother Fred who died in 1926 at age 39.

Pietro Mutto wears sports attire in this photograph. He was 45 when he died in 1919.

Poldina Gavello *was only 20 years old when she passed away in 1916.*
This photograph shows classic studio portraiture with right side lighting that highlights the delicate contours of her face. Holding a bouquet, wearing an ornate locket, earrings and a flower in her hair, Poldina presents an impressive figure.

Lorenzo Nanni
Note Lorenzo's pocket protector, hat, beard and the buggy in the background.

John Flora
John poses with a model of a ship and displays the flag of the United States yachting insignia.

1868 – 1918   Age 50

Died October 3, 1925

Cesarina Papera Quilici
1884 — 1905   Age 21
Cesarina displays a wavy hairstyle popular at the turn of the century.

The portrait of **Mariiana Taddei** *demonstrates unusual photo selection that creates an atypical effect. Mariiana died at age 7 in 1923.*

Mannuel Nava
February 14, 1893 — December 26, 1909
Born in Mazatlan, Mexico, died at age 16.

Rosina D'Antonio
Born in Palermo, Italy in 1886, died at 36 in 1922.

The Patania Family pose for this family portrait.
Father Carmelo, 1885 — 1978,
Mother Nunziati 1891 — 1931
Permina 1912 — 1931.

Permina, age 19, and Nunziati, age 40, both died on August 30, 1931.

Giovanina and Alice De Tomasi

Giovanina (left) born in Milan, was 25 when she died in 1918 .
Alice, curls galore, was born June 6 of the same year. She died March 30, 1925 at age 6.

Fornaciari and Elio Raffaello

Fornaciari (left) was born in Porcari, Italy in 1885 and died in San
Francisco in 1927. Elio was born in 1918 and died in 1920.

Mother and Daughter

Paolina Repetto, *"an exemplary mother of elevated principles" died in 1910 at age 58. Her "most affectionate" daughter* **Agata** *lived just two more years and died age 27 in 1912.*

Leona Amaroso, *shown here in uniform, died in 1943 during the middle of World War II.*

Angelina Uccelli *was 7 when she passed away in 1917. She poses hands clasped, head tilted and staring straight into the camera.*

Bartollo Biscotto

1863 – 1923   Age 60

*Bartollo pictured here at a younger age in the uniform of a Bersaglieri –
Italy's "shock troops" usually the first into battle. His last name translates
as "biscuit" in English.*

Attilio Quartararo *1908 — 1917*
Attilio carries a book and wears a thigh-length
sweater with full pockets as he poses near a stone wall.

Guilio E. Lazzerini *1921 — 1934*
Whose inscription tells us his early death
"deeply affected his parents."

Emanuel and Victoria Usberti
Emanuel — *May 21, 1894 to Dec. 29, 1949*
Victoria — *March 5, 1890 to April 22, 1930*
The Usberti's assume a more casual posture in
this formal portrait conveying a personal touch.

Sarah Feliciano
August 3, 1926 to September 26, 1931
Sarah wears bobbed hair and a ribbon on her blouse.
She stares straight into the camera eschewing a
smile but fostering a sense of personal presence.

The La Rocca Family

Both tragedy and amusement are represented by the portraits of this family. Salvatore's portrait supplies unusual and entertaining imagery for a memoriam. The story regarding the other members of his family regrettably depicts a devastating period in our nation's history.

Right: **Salvatore La Rocca** *died in San Francisco on Feb 11., 1920 at the age of 29. He wears full "cowboy" regalia including full length sheepskin chaps.*

The 1918 Spanish Flu Epidemic *claimed the lives of all the members of the La Rocca family below.*

Concetta, wife and mother, died first on November 4, 1918 at age 31. Daughter Stella died next on November 6, 1918 at age 4. Antonio, the father, died on November 9, 1918 at age 43.
Rosie joined them all on November 20, 1918 at age 8.

Postmortem Photographs from the Italian Cemetery

Seven postmortems have been confirmed in the Italian Cemetery in Colma. A postmortem portrait of twins on a tombstone is extremely rare, possibly one-of-a-kind.

- A Rare Postmortem of Twins -

The Baiochhi Brothers

*Gino (above right) and **Aldo** (left) **Baiocchi** were both born on July 5, 1928 and died eleven months later and three days apart on June 2 and May 31, 1929 respectively.*

Leonardo Magnoli
Born in San Francisco on April 27, 1917.
He died on February 17, 1918 at the age of 10 months.

Vincenzo Pieri was 17 months old when he died in 1910. His eyes are still open in this postmortem picture. Children were often placed in the photo as if still sleeping.

Pietro Marino was 59 when he died in 1905. His example is unusual because Pietro's eyes remain open in his post mortem photograph. This was done intentionally to present the subject's last remaining image as he was in life.

Orazio Ortissi was just under two years of age when he died in 1926. This post mortem shows him in his coffin.

Giovanni Caramatti
June 23, 1918 to March 27, 1919.
Note his carefully interlaced fingers.

CHAPTER SEVEN

Photo-Ceramic Memorial Portraiture as an Art Form

For those readers already convinced that photo-ceramic memorial portraiture is a legitimate art form possessing authentic historical value, Chapters 7 and 8 may seem unnecessary. But they also may enrich your understanding. They are a response to sources who told me that these portraits do not constitute art, that their utilitarian function limits them to the status of a funerary addendum, a mere gravestone accessory. Critics also maintained that, because memorial portraits are not mentioned in history books, they cannot be considered genuine historical artifacts. I believe that an inadequate assessment of their role in our culture. This and the following chapter attempt to convey my perspective.

Art is defined as the application of skill and taste to the production of beauty by imitation or design. The genesis of every memorial portrait is a photograph, which can be either art or documentation. A memorial portrait may be mounted on a gravestone but it is born a photograph. It originates as art.

Often designed and crafted by European artisans, these objects represent a singular form of popular art. Their concave and oval profile, often encircled in gold, gives them a distinctive appearance. Blending the sciences of photography, chemistry and physics, they produce appealing images made to last.

The memorial artisan often also performed detailed and extensive retouching of the original picture before reproducing it with precious metals, encasing it in resin and firing it in the kiln. These memorial portraits required craftsmen who understood chemistry, physics and possessed the eye of an artist.

An Ancient Art Form

Portraiture, the art of transferring a person's face to some medium, represents one of the oldest forms of art. The ancient Greeks perfected the process of reproducing faces on two-dimensional media. The first to incorporate faces of their rulers onto coin, they pioneered the use of perspective to present their subjects in an accurate yet flattering manner. The Egyptians preceded the Greeks with portraits on flat surfaces but enjoyed less success re-creating realistic perspective.

Nineteenth-century photographers often used negatives as large as the human face. This produced images with remarkable detail. Mina Maffei's studio portrait (p. 46) represents an excellent example.

Photography's earliest efforts honored the human face. By controlling lighting, angle and depth of field the professional photographer helped working men and women appear regal and stately. Add a dramatic pose, a scenic backdrop and the typical low-income laborer possessed a permanent representation of his or her image that pleased and flattered forever.

Just as the Romans copied the Greeks to idealize Emperor Augustus' profile and employ his coins as propaganda to unify his empire, the portrait photographer of the early 20th century created long-lasting images for personal marketing. With the subjects appearing at their very best, a photograph could be mailed across the country to a prospective beau or anxious family wondering what became of their son or daughter. Fears were assuaged. Marriages were made. Photography proliferated. Today it permeates our digital culture in a myriad of forms and function.

Portraiture seeks to represent the optimum portrayal of its subject. It has succeeded for millennia. Memorial portraiture makes this statement an enduring one.

Portraits Equal More Than the Sum of Their Parts

Portraits speak the language of symbols. When we see the formal photograph of Marko Rado, holding his crutch so prominently, we feel his pride, we understand the message he wanted to convey. His portrait and epitaph, "Leg buried 1928, Marko Rado 1891 – 1947," (p. 38) tell us much about Rado and how he wanted to be perceived. Rado interred his leg 19 years before he joined his limb in repose. He wanted us to know it was important to him

This collection of photo-ceramic portraiture represents art with a purpose. The portraits commemorate the working class and the middle class. They confirm our common bond. They acknowledge individuals who lived this phase of America's melting pot history. In doing so, they bond art with history.

Our Face: Unique and Timeless Symbol of Our Being

If pictures are worth a thousand words, these portraits can be considered the final chapter of someone's life. Each of our faces is unique. Countless nuances allow us to express without words. One smile elicits another. A frown generates distance. Our face conveys our individuality at a subjective level few can explain but all understand.

Our face greets the world everywhere we go. It portrays our every emotion, conscious or not, intentional or not. Our face causes others to recognize, admire or avoid us. It communicates beyond the boundaries of our bodies. As these portraits demonstrate, a face can reach across time and tell other eras who we were. We know the person through their portrait. We sense who they are. They make us think. They make us feel. It is art at its best.

The ancient portrait of Cleopatra from 40 B.C. graces a silver coin from the author's private collection and demonstrates the ancient roots of the art of portraiture. (Picture is 3X actual size.)

CHAPTER EIGHT

Photo-Ceramic Memorial Portraits as Artifacts

An artifact is a tool or ornament possessing archaeological or cultural interest. Artifacts impart important information about the past and the people who lived at that time.

Memorial portraits preserve images of people, places, fashion and style. They depict buildings and objects, private and public, from their era. In many cases, specifically postmortem portraits of children, they may preserve the only existing photograph of their subject.[9] They contain fragments of human history that otherwise might be lost forever. They link people from the past with us in the present and preserve them for the future. That is the nature of an artifact.

Most of these portraits depict individuals from the lower and middle classes. They were not revered in history books or lectured about in schools. They were people who lived lives much like our own. This makes their portraits meaningful to us. We can relate to them. They lived much as we do, day to day, working, growing up, marrying, having children and dying. Some never experienced many of those milestones. Life's valued moments are captured and preserved. They represent an unheralded but important adjunct to our understanding of the times in which they lived and died.

During the first 30 years of the 20th century, photographs were not as available as they are today. For children under 12, there may have been only one or two family photographs from which to select a memorial portrait. This sometimes forced families to retouch family photos to eliminate family members and isolate the child in the photo. Or they used casual snapshots as their memorial, providing us glimpses into their everyday life. The collection in *Forgotten Faces* demonstrates these informal times – subjects leaning playfully against a wall, in their backyard or surrounded by scenes from the city they visited on vacation or perhaps called home.

Memorial Portraits as Time Capsules

Alone the portraits depict individual instants in time and place. They relate private stories about a particular person or family. Collectively, the portraits provide insights into our culture and ancestry. They bring to light authentic images of immigrants from 28 nations. These men, women and children lived and died during some of the most turbulent and important periods of our history – the turn of the 20th century, World War I, the Roaring Twenties, the Great Depression and much of World War II.

---

[9] Dr. Stanley B.Burns, *Death in America*

Nations from Southern and Eastern Europe, Latin America, China, Russia and the Philippines are represented in the portraits of Holy Cross. The portraits affirm that America is indeed a nation of immigrants. We meet the people who migrated to California, leaving their mark on our landscape as well as our collective psyche.

History Comes Alive Through These Portals to the Past...

This face-to-face encounter is most evident in the stories of Bridie Kearney, James Kendrick and Benjamin Root. Through circumstances beyond their control, their lives made newspaper headlines that we rediscover decades later in the archives of the San Francisco Chronicle and the Examiner.

The Story of Bridie Kearney

The newspaper headlines of February 27, 1928, (p. 32) shouted the story across the front page: "Girl Shot to Death at Wedding Party." Bridie Kearney, a native of Cork, Ireland, was mysteriously shot in the head at the age of 24. Witnesses at the wedding party on Sutter and Divisadero streets in San Francisco included her brother Patrick and fiancé John Keane, who was wounded. They identified Lloyd Groat, a San Francisco policeman, as having fired the shot that killed Ms. Kearney. They agreed that Bridie was leaving the hall with other guests when she was shot through the temple with a bullet from Officer Groat's revolver. Keane received a flesh wound in the forehead from the same bullet. The gun was found in the gutter with a single shot fired from its otherwise empty chamber. Groat claimed the gun was taken from his holster in a struggle and he never held it in his hand. Several witnesses said "a man in a gray overcoat" fired the shot. Officer Groat was wearing a gray overcoat and gray suit.

During the course of the trial, witnesses often contradicted each other as to whether Groat actually fired his gun. Some, including Betty Kearney, initially claimed it was Groat's partner, Walter Salisbury, who fired the shot. These contradictions later proved critical in the jury's verdict. Groat and Salisbury claimed they were trying to break up a fight when Groat's gun somehow disappeared. Kearney warned, "They will try to cover this up. I know they will." She was in the hall at the time of the shooting.

When other witnesses recanted original testimony regarding Groat, he was acquitted of the crime and instructed to report back to duty. There were no other suspects and no one was ever convicted of the shooting. Officer Groat was ordered to return to work, but four months later, he retired from the San Francisco Police Department without explanation. He later made it into the newspapers again when he was arrested twice in 1929 for possession of liquor, then still illegal under Prohibition.

Bridget is buried with a child just under two years of age, Padriac Pearse Cotter, who died a few months after her on June 4, 1928. Padriac is named after an Irish poet known for his revolutionary perspectives. The relationship between the two is not known.

The Story of James Kendrick

James Kendrick (p. 34) was a private in the U.S. 363rd Infantry, a veteran of World War I where he fought in France. World War I created the term "trench warfare." "After the Battle of the Marne in September 1914, the Germans were forced to retreat to the River Aisne. The German commander, General Erich von Falkenhayn, decided that his troops must at all costs hold onto those parts of France and Belgium that Germany still occupied. Falkenhayn ordered his men to dig trenches that would provide them with protection from the advancing French and British troops. The Allies soon realized that they could not break through this line and they also began to dig trenches. After a few months these trenches had spread from the North Sea to the Swiss Frontier." [10]

Pvt. James Kendrick "went over the top" of the trenches to attack the German enemy eight times in France and survived "without a scratch," according to his Army buddies. He was reported to be the first member of the 363rd Infantry welcomed back to America by San Francisco Mayor "Sunny" Jim Rolph.

Ironically, on May 25, 1919, soon after Kendrick's return to San Francisco, he was shot and killed by a San Francisco policeman, John Kelly. Kendrick was 25 years old when he was killed as he and six of friends from the 363rd Infantry were partying at the Eureka Café on Cortland Avenue. They got a bit boisterous and Officer Kelly was called to the café to calm them down. Kelly claimed he was set upon by the group and only fired in self-defense. Kendrick's friends disputed this and said Kendrick was nine feet away when Kelly opened fire. "It would not have been so bad," said one of them, "if Jimmy had been bumped off while serving his country, strafing the Hun; but to be finished off by a cop when all he was trying to do was explain. Gee, that's a bit too much." – San Francisco Chronicle, May 30, 1919.

Mayor Rolph ordered an inquiry into the shooting. The investigation revealed that no powder marks were found on Kendrick's clothes, proving Kendrick was not near Kelley when Kelly shot him. Kelly was subsequently found guilty of manslaughter. More than 1,000 uniformed soldiers from the 363rd Infantry attended Kendrick's funeral at Holy Cross Cemetery; an estimated twice that many civilians participated in the private's final rites.

---

[10] Martin Gilbert *The First World War* – excerpt from The National Archives *Learning Curve*

The Kendrick family suffered the loss of many family members at very early ages. Four sons and two daughters all died before they reached 35. Pvt. Kendrick's brother William died in 1914 at age 21. James died in 1919. His brother Peter died at 18 in 1924. His 25-year-old brother, John, died in 1926. His sister Rose was 30 when she died in 1927, and sister May died in 1928 at age 33. Their father, Michael Kendrick, was 80 when he died in 1923. The mother of the family is not listed on the headstone.

The Story of Benjamin Root

San Francisco police Officer Benjamin Root (p. 33) was found at Ninth and Brannan streets in San Francisco on the last day of March 1926, entangled in the wreckage of his motorcycle. He died of those injuries the following afternoon on April 1, at age 27. Root was "still astride his machine" with his feet tangled in the wheels and his hat 20 feet away.

According to newspaper reports, Root was known by his fellow officers as an "unusually careful rider." His sudden death surprised them. They opened an investigation into whether he was a hit-and-run victim or had been chasing a speeding driver. The investigation was inconclusive and details of how he died were never confirmed. It was later surmised that repairs to nearby train tracks may have created unavoidable hazards in the streets and caused Root's accident.

Root joined the SFPD in 1924 after several years as a San Francisco fireman. Born in Centerville, Iowa, in 1898, he left behind his pregnant wife, Helen, and two children, 8 and 5 years old. The Hearst-owned San Francisco Examiner raised more than $1,275 for the family and hundreds attended the officer's funeral. Helen, though remarried, was buried with Benjamin, 61 years later. Benjamin's portrait shows him posed on his motorcycle with a San Francisco neighborhood in the background. This tombstone photograph tells us a lot about Benjamin, as it was intended to do.

The portraits reflect a lifetime in a single image. Each story behind each face shelters a private yet valued history. As artifacts, the portraits bring light and life to a history lost in the shadows of time and death.

What the Statistics of the Era Tell Us About Our Sample

The Holy Cross collection does not represent a formal scientific inquiry into the subject. However, the statistics and the stories behind the portraits provide a glimpse into this tumultuous era of American history. Gravestone inscriptions often reveal information easily overlooked or obscured by the passage of time. The portraits of Holy

Cross yield mysteries, misfortune and an era not unlike our own – full of confusing and challenging change within a rapidly evolving society. Tales of immigrant families come to light after a century of living in shadows. Statistical evidence of hardship becomes apparent for children and those in the prime of their lives as well.

A report by the U.S. Department of Health and Human Services' Office on Women's Health, in April 2002, provides a somber assessment of life expectancy during this era. "In 1900, 30 percent of infants in America's major cities died before their first birthdays. The average life expectancy for an American woman was 48.3 years. (Life expectancy for men was 47.8.) Infectious diseases, including pneumonia, influenza, tuberculosis and syphilis, were the leading causes of death for men, women and children. The maternal mortality rate was 6 to 9 deaths per 1,000 live births. Ninety percent of children were born at home. Some births went unattended; others were attended by midwives or doctors who were often poorly trained. In 1900, only 10% of the nation's physicians attended college. The portraits of Holy Cross mirror these statistics in many ways.

Of the 500 portraits catalogued, 29% represent children under 12 years of age. Another 15% are 19 and younger. Fully 40% of the Holy Cross portraits from 1899 to 1945 document the deaths of people younger than 20.

Adults 20 to 30 years old yield another 22%. People younger than 30 compose 66% of the portraits. Two out of every three people shown in these portraits never celebrated their 30th birthday. Another 20% are people in their 30s, and only 14% are over 40 years of age.

Age at death	% of Sample
1-12	*29*
13-19	*15*
20-29	*22*
30-40	*20*
40+	*14*

The Holy Cross Sample
500 Memorial Portraits by Age Group

Children under 12 represent the largest age group in the sample of 500 Holy Cross portraits. It is likely that parents of young children were more motivated than others to preserve their children's image. People under the age of 30 represent almost two thirds of the sample. Although this sample does not represent any statistical relevance to the wider population, it does underscore that during the early decades of 20th century, the young died early and often.

These data are not scientific. They have no statistical relevance. It is likely that parents of children felt more motivated to leave behind a portrait because little else remained to commemorate the child. We cannot make population-wide deductions from this information. That said, some conclusions are worth noting.

Cause of Death

The portraits tell us that from 1900 to 1940 the young died early and often. Though penicillin was discovered in 1928, practical application did not become widespread until World War II. Diphtheria, tuberculosis, rabies, hepatitis, poliomyelitis and smallpox spread easily in cities and frequently resulted in death.[11]

Even mumps, measles and the flu could prove fatal. In 1918, the worldwide epidemic of influenza killed 500,000 Americans – more than died in World War I, World War II, the Korean War and the Vietnam War combined. Celebrating the end of the First World War, 30,000 San Franciscans literally took to the streets to dance and celebrate. By law, they all wore face masks. When the first sirens sounded in November 1918 to signal it was legal and safe to remove protective face masks, more than 2,100 people in San Francisco had died of the flu.

Holy Cross set aside a section for those who died of the flu during this time. Children, teenagers and healthy young adults succumbed to influenza and other transmittable diseases at a time when doctors possessed few remedies.

Cemetery archives show tuberculosis producing one of the highest death rates among our sample. Entire families, even over the span of years, died from TB. Pulmonary problems, including pneumonia, represent the largest category for cause of death. "Failures of the heart" in a variety of manifestations – arteriosclerosis and even "fatty heart" are frequently listed as cause of death. Children died of malnutrition, were crushed by heavy objects and succumbed to infections that antibiotics routinely cure today.

---

[11] National Office of Vital Statistics 1947

Adults died of "wounds to the heart," extensive burns and spinal meningitis. But they also passed away from diagnoses that today seem obscure – "insanity," epileptic convulsions, consumption and diarrhea. The name of death has changed, but the images of its constant presence remain in these portals into the past.

The portraits do not show us the "cause of death" of their subjects. Instead they represent artifacts with a human face. Sometimes, history is best understood that way. For this alone, the portraits deserve their proper place in our collective memory.

The McAffery angel stands guard in one of the most remote areas of Holy Cross Cemetery. Nearby the graves of James Kendrick, Ana Yberra, James Curtin and the Gracieux sisters rest under his protective presence.

Photo-Gallery IV
From the Photo-Archives of Richard E. Meyer

Greek Orthodox Archbishop - 1939

Professor Meyer provides photographs from his private archive of over 20,000 photographs of cemeteries and funerary arts. These photos take us to the mid-western and western United States and across the Pacific to Hawaii. His images also bring us to France and offer some rare, unusual and beautiful examples of the art form.

A Distinctive Family Portrait

This family stone from America's heartland contains two unusual portraits. On the left, the family is gathered outdoors for a group portrait. Group photographs on tombstones are atypical. This one includes seven people and is dated 1945.

On the same stone is a portrait (below) containing a collage of photographs and Christian images. The man in the center is surrounded by loved ones and depictions of Christ. The family photos beneath the man each have the person's name hand-written underneath the pictures.

The portrait showing the family posed outdoors appears to contain all the same people as the collage below. The individual figures in the collage photos seem to be about five years younger than those in the family gathering, at least as far as the children are concerned. The man in the center may have used a much earlier picture of himself in the collage as he and his wife look considerably older there than in the family photo. These two distinctive portraits on a single stone constitute a highly individualized style and approach to memorial portraits.

Massacrées

This stone from d'Oradour-sur-Glane, France describes the massacre of these four young girls "par les hordes nazie's"[by Nazi hoards] on June 10, 1944. Their names and ages are shown below their pictures.

This man wears a white tie with a fedora hat and an expression to match. He died in 1937.

This lawyer from Nice, France is dressed in his court robes. He died in 1924 at the age of 30.

This portrait shows a midwestern husband and wife involved in a book. The image conveys a sense of mutuality, which they probably intended. It is dated 1935.

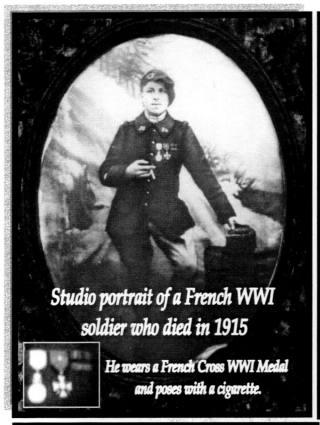

Studio portrait of a French WWI
soldier who died in 1915

He wears a French Cross WWI Medal
and poses with a cigarette.

A studio portrait of an American
WWI soldier who died in 1918

Chicago Policeman - 1925

The bottom of his portrait reveals a "Dedo" insignia.

WWII Avaitor, USA, 1944

Portraits that Tell Stories About their Subjects

Family members often select portrait photos that convey their loved ones special qualities or interests.

The man, who died in 1938, holds a trumpet. The bottom of this photo also reveals a "Dedo" signature on its portrait.

America's West was defined by men on horseback. This Oregon man proudly displays his love of the outdoors and equestrian pastimes. He died in 1948.

The French are known to love their dogs. The family of this woman from Vence, sought to reveal her close relationship with her pet dog by choosing this photo of them together for her memorial portrait.

She also wears a large fur coat and plumed hat. She died in 1934.

Memorial Portraits from Hawaii

This man was the son of a reverend.
He was born on Oahu and died on Maui on July 4, 1910 at the age of 21.

Mother and Infant
The child, Susie, died in 1910 at the age of 2.
Her mother, Elisa, died at the age of 40 in 1924.

This Wisconsin girl poses in her First Holy Communion veil, dress and shoes next to a lighted candle. She died in 1923.

The sign in the background proudly dates this Chicago boy's First Holy Communion. He died just 7 years later in 1931.

Heartland, USA

This US soldier from WW I poses for his seated photo holding his hat in his lap and his hand to his cheek. He died in 1917 and is from the midwest.

This bride holds a bouquet and wears a full-length diaphanous veil with her wedding gown. She died in 1928.

Postmortems from the Collection of Richard E. Meyer

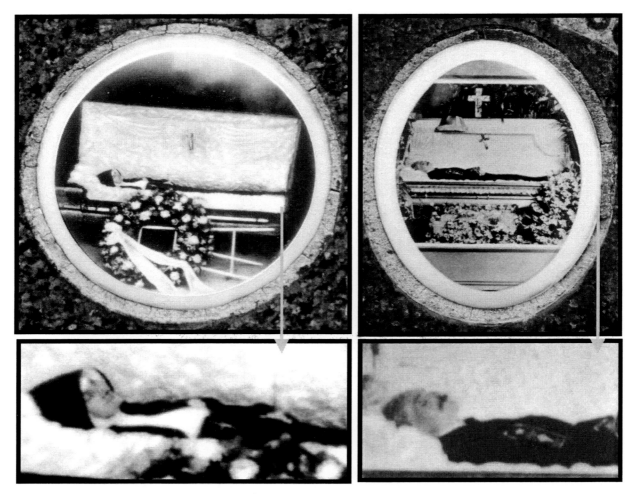

This postmortem portrait shows a nun dressed in full habit lying in her coffin. She died in 1941.

This portrait shows a mid-western man in his coffin. He died in 1943.

This postmortem shows a French child who died in 1933 at the age of five. "Our Small One – Beloved"

From the Photo Collection of Cathy Ward
The Face of the German Soldier – WWI & WWII

This airman wears the Luftwaffe Signal Corps collar tabs on his lapel.

Photo-ceramic portraits preserve history through imagery. Many portraits, such as those of young children, evoke emotion. The memorial portraits of Cathy Ward also elicit an emotional response. As Cathy describes these faces from WWI and WWII taken in Bavaria: "they are the faces of war seldom seen — those of the aggressors — young German soldiers from the disgraced Germany of two World Wars."

Note: some portraits have had surnames digitally obscured to protect the privacy of their subjects and modern relations.

The Face of the German Soldier: World War I—Three Brothers

Johann
Died 1915 at age 32

The brothers' headstone with epitaphs.

Anton
Died 1916 at age 21

Hubert
Died 1917 at age 27

Georg
Died at age 33

The headstone of Georg and Stefan

"In remembrance of the fallen brothers"

Note: some photos on this page had some ceramic reflections digitally lightened. The original portraits were not altered in any way.

**Three Brothers –
Three Hats.**
Top Left: *wears a cap and smokes a pipe.*
Top Right: *wears a Third Reich Army Enlisted Dress Hat.*
Bottom: *wears a standard issue German infantry helmet.*

Peter
"Remembering Our Dear Son"
Peter died in the Ukraine on July 7, 1941 at the age of 21.
He wears a flight helmet and goggles.

Three Brothers

Karl was born December 16, 1909.
He died in February 9, 1942 in Russia.

Karl
Tischlermstr.v. Karlsbad-Kohlhau
geb.16.12.1909 Uffz. ein.Jnf-Sturmabt.
gef.9.2.1942 bei Sitshoje-Russland
Johann
Bauer aus Vollmau-Langlammitz
geb.16.6.1910 gef.7.7.1944 bei Stalino
Heinrich
Musiker u.Bauer aus Langlammitz
geb.28.9.1910 vermißt seit 28.1.1943
bei Kursk-Kastorroje

Heinrich wears a Third Reich
Army Officer's Dress Hat.
He died in 1943 at age 32.
He was a musician and farmer.

Born on June 16, 1910
Johann died January 28, 1943.

Johann and Heinrich both wear the German eagle holding a swastika — the symbol of National Socialism.

Examples of the Memorial Portraits in other U.S. Locations from the Collection of Ron Horne

An Unusual Postmortem with a Hidden Story

This rare postmortem portrait from a cemetery in Pennsylvania shows a young boy standing beside a deceased child lying in the coffin to his right. The ribbon on the flowers bears the Italian phrase "Nostro Fratello" – our brother. The child died in 1925 at age 4.

The picture of the smiling boy was added afterwards to the postmortem photograph in this retouched composite. Laurel Gabel, AGS member and lecturer, adds, "I've seen more than one postmortem (not on a gravestone) where the child is shown in death and -- added in, as in your example -- in life. Could the standing figure be the same child in life?"

- portrait found with the assistance of Robert Di Benedetto

This man was 26 when he died in 1943. An American serviceman of Greek descent, he poses in front of a fountain with an ancient Greek style temple in the background.

This interesting choice of photos represents a man who died in 1943 at the age of 75. He wears a three piece suit while reading a newspaper.

This "Beloved Mother, Wife and Daughter" was 23 when she died in 1944. She wears dark colors with no jewelry.

This woman was 86 when she died in 1944. With striking simplicity, she wears a white head covering with a buttoned, ribbed sweater. Her photo bears the signature "Stola" in small letters at the bottom of the portrait.

This stately portrait was found in a rural California cemetery.

Rural cemeteries yield interesting memorial portraits.

Pauline died in 1946 at the age of 65. This younger photograph of her shows another example of "mise-en-abime" – a portrait within a portrait. Like Annie Corcoran on page 39, Pauline wears the portrait of an absent loved one on her broach. Her married surname is Italian. This photo was found in a small, rural cemetery in northern California. How many unusual and beautiful portraits remain undiscovered in rural cemeteries, large and small, across America?

This seated woman was 44 when she died in 1943. Her hairstyle indicates her picture was taken sometime in the twenties.

This woman was 49 when she died in 1944. She wears a mourning shawl in the Greek tradition.

This soldier died in 1937 at the age of 42. He wears spectacles without shafts and sports a thin mustache.

This man died in 1940 at the age of 30. He wears a high-collared uniform and soft cap.

This California portrait shows a Major General from the Russian Army. He was born in Sitka Alaska, Russia in 1865. Two years later, the United States purchased Alaska from Russia for 7.2 million dollars. The general died in San Francisco in 1936 at age 71. He displays six separate medals on his uniform.

Sisters

Elsa on the left and Lia on the right look to the left of the camera at the encouragement of the photographer who posed them with props appropriate to their ages: a book and short table. The girls died just two weeks apart in the spring of 1916, Elsa at age 3 and Lia age 7.

Note the retouching – lightening – of the floor around the girls' shoes separating them from the color of the floor. Both girls wear white dresses, lockets and ankle-belted shoes for the occasion.

CHAPTER NINE

Immigration in San Francisco and California: 1900 – 1940

The portraits of *Forgotten Faces* emerged at the dawn of the 20th century as Anthony O'Brien was passing away in 1899 at the age of 41. Anthony's portrait (p. 42, 155) is the oldest in Holy Cross Cemetery. It is also the oldest in any of Colma's cemeteries. O'Brien's and the other 500 portraits there span a 45-year period that includes two world wars and ends with Germany's surrender in 1945. It was an era of major immigration to the United States and the West Coast. This period transformed the economy and culture of San Francisco and California.

In 1906, San Francisco was devastated by an earthquake and ensuing fire. That same year, as told to us by the portraits, 31-year-old Ignacio Vukovich celebrated the birth of his son, Mate (p. 162). Remember their names and their story. Four years later, as San Francisco was busily rebuilding itself, Antonita Gracieux (p. 45) passed away at age 7. Her sister Maria was three at the time. 1910 was also the year Maria Ghiberla (p. 160) lost her 22-year-old son, August. Furthermore, it was the year Angel Island – Ellis Island's West Coast counterpart – began housing Chinese immigrants under the newly reinforced Chinese Exclusion Act. For the next 30 years, this 740-acre island served as the West Coast gateway for a rapidly expanding immigrant population. It was a major occasion in California's history while Antonita and August passed from the scene with only their families and friends taking notice.

World War I began in August 1914. Events turned uncertain and chaotic. In December 1915, 18-year-old Selena Perez (p. 47) became ill and died, leaving her 13-year-old sister, Lucy, behind. In 1916, angry longshoremen went on strike, freezing San Francisco's ports, bringing international shipping to a halt for three months. A saga of sadness was only beginning for the Perez family but the headlines never noticed.

Even so, the Spanish Flu of 1918 raged on as if a world war alone did not generate enough tragedy for human kind. Tragically representing the devastation of this pandemic event, the mother, father and two young daughters of the La Rocca family (p. 114) all died in the month of November, 1918 of the disease.

Laborers began migrating to America's big cities during this era. Incoming immigrants clashed with established union labor at bustling San Francisco ports, where products and people were arriving from the Far East, South America as well as the East Coast at a record pace. Unions and immigrants clashed over jobs.

World War I ended in 1918. America celebrated. San Francisco Mayor "Sunny" Jim Rolph settled comfortably into the second of his five terms. His long reign facilitated an infusion of economic growth to the Bay Area. In 1919, four years after her sister Selena's death, Lucy Perez also succumbed to illness at the age of 17. While the world focused on the beginning and the end of its first world war, Maria and Theodore Perez grieved the loss of both their teenage daughters.

The year of the much-heralded Seattle General Strike – 1919 – 10-year-old Gustove Grialou (p. 161) died suddenly. Months later, and nine years after the death of her sister Antonita, Maria Gracieux joined her in death at the age of 13. The Gracieux sisters (p. 45) were buried in their shared grave in a remote corner of Holy Cross' broad valley grounds. History records the actions of striking longshoremen; memorial portraits preserve a quieter but equally relevant history.

Construction on many of San Francisco's most famous landmarks now occurred at an explosive rate. A year after Lupe Vera (p. 168) was born in 1914, the beautiful Palace of Fine Arts was completed. Built for the Panama-Pacific Expedition and World's Fair, it signified an era of architectural growth. San Francisco subsequently initiated its multi-tiered City Hall, symbolic Coit Tower and then the iconoclastic Golden Gate Bridge in 1933. Lupe Vera, with her movie star looks, witnessed it all before dying in 1937 at the young age of 23. City Hall, Coit Tower and the Golden Gate Bridge still stand testament to that time. But only Lupe's portrait remains to tell her story.

During that time the Roaring Twenties sounded long and loud on the West Coast. Sunny Jim's mayoral road to the governor's office escalated Prohibition and red-light profits into a booming underground economy. Such excess made San Francisco a formidable representative of the raucous era. As the decade roared forward it took some of its celebrants in the prime of their lives.

From the Middle East, Kahlil (Syria) and Philomena Warris (Lebanon), lost their 22-year-old son Joseph (p. 41) in February 1920. He was buried near Lucy and Selena Perez. Recalling the birth of Mate Vukovich in 1906 when San Francisco experienced its historic earthquake, 1921 now marks the year of Mate's death (p. 162) at only 15. His father, Ignacio, lived on without Mate until 1935, when he died at 59. Ignacio came to America from Czechoslovakia and at the age of 41 buried his teenage son in the soil of his new country.

In 1922, as the notorious era gathered momentum, Maria Perez, 50, now followed her two daughters, Selena and Lucy (p. 47) in death. Theodore Perez, once husband and father, faced the second decade of the new century alone; 13 years later in 1935, at age 66, he was buried with his wife and daughters.

Elvira Russett, 33, Catherine Elich, 22, (p. 43) and Constance Mora, 15, (p. 42) had their lives cut short as the Twenties roared on without them. Defendante Guerra, 21, Libertante Terrananova, 19, Bessie Wong, 24, and Minna Maffei, 19, (p. 46) were all cut down before their chance to bloom. Bernard Pressans, James Curtin and Joseph Murphy (p. 76) all died in their teens before they could participate in this decade of flappers, bootleg whiskey and mob rule.

As the decade moved toward conclusion, more portraits were mounted on the tombstones at Holy Cross. Thirty-three-year-old Rose Rauschan (p. 160), a Hungarian native, died in 1927, leaving behind her 15-year-old son, Paul. Without her, his life would not be long. The well-dressed Camille Lutich (p. 159) died in 1928 before turning 21. Her father, Andrew, had died nine years earlier, also before his time. He was 34 when he passed away in 1917. Quietly, and beyond the din of daily news, Rose Lombardi (p. 70) surrendered to illness in 1929. She was 9.

The decade of the Twenties, whose signature is the sound of wild lions, produced an aura that survived it for generations. Many from that era, whose portraits speak from Holy Cross today, remained at the edge of its shadow, their stories lost in the tumult of the times.

At this time, politics, as always, took center stage. Mayor Rolph, with federal help, tried to diminish the power of the unions. His efforts for a time lessened the influence of the unions, whose power eventually resurfaced again after World War II.

"Waves" of Immigrants Enter the United States

In 1921, 9-year-old Alice Portos (p. 71) and 29-year-old fireman Anthony Mello (p. 35) both passed away. Within a year the Supreme Court reaffirmed that Asian immigrants could not become U.S. citizens. This ruling perpetuated the love-hate relationship San Francisco maintained for its large, hard-working Asian immigrant population. First- and second-generation East Coast immigrants moved West, seeking refuge from the overcrowded cities back there, where poor services, inadequate water supplies, subsistence living and rampant disease characterized immigrant life in the slums.

Russians, Polish, Irish and, in larger numbers, Italians headed West to California. Known as the "third wave" of immigration,[12] they differed from the predominantly British and German immigrants in the early 1900s. Mostly from Southern and Eastern Europe, they spoke little or no English. The cultural differences between new immigrants and the established "first wave" – 1820 to 1860 and "second wave" - 1860 to 1890 – populations created constant friction and palpable tension in crowded San Francisco tenements.

Even so, the economy thrived because affordable labor accompanied by technological progress increased America's productivity. From 1919 through 1929 the output of American workers increased 43% through mass production techniques. The nation's economy expanded at a prolific rate. The upper- and middle-classes prospered and even unskilled laborers enhanced their quality of life in measurable ways.

However, in 1929, San Francisco, along with the rest of the nation, plummeted from the giddy heights of economic expansion to the depths of financial ruin. That same year, Dorothy Kristolovich and her son Joseph (p. 50) both died during childbirth. Some disasters are so loud that others are barely heard above the din.

The historic crash of the stock market heralded the country's Great Depression. Within a few months, more than 100,000 companies were forced to close; 100 times that number of American workers found themselves suddenly jobless. Americans' purchasing power dropped through the floor.

The Bay Area revived economically when it built its two great bridges, the first in 1933. That was the year that Ermanno Parensi (p. 163) and his wife, Declinda, died, both at age 73. The Parensis were in the prime of their lives as the new century was born and struggled forward. They came to their end before these famous bridges carried a single car across their spans. In 1933, Paul Rauschan, (p. 160) whose Hungarian-born mother died in 1927 when he was 15, followed her prematurely eight years later.

The Thirties saw the region's economy expand as new building kept much-needed capital flowing into the area. This created a new monetary lifeline for Northern California. The linkage of the Bay's bridges lifted San Francisco into a dynamic marketplace, sustaining it – though not without many destabilizing fluctuations – throughout the thirties and into the opening volleys of World War II.

---

[12] Jonathan Lee and Robert Siemborski, *The American Immigration Home Page*
http://www.bergen.org/AAST/Projects/Immigration/

As the thirties began, memorial portraits marked sadder milestones without deference to the age of the subjects. Francis Bzik (p. 169), a native of Yugoslavia, died at 55 in 1930. Maria Lino (p. 173) was 69 when she died in 1931, while Anita Lopez (p. 77) barely turned 4 before she passed. Jose Bermudez (p. 171), posing proudly in his portrait, died at 29 in 1932. Forty-three-year-old Manual Pegueros, husband to then-19-year-old Lupe Vera, died in 1933. As noted previously, Lupe lived only four more years before falling ill and dying at age 23.

Stefina Tocker, 29, (p. 43) shown in her memorial portrait with full fur, pearls and handbag ready for an evening on the town, was available for no more galas after 1934. One year-olds Myrna Lee (p. 78) and Mary Bugeja (p. 81) followed her in 1935. Rosaria Reta (p. 78), just 5 years old, joined them in Holy Cross Children's Perpetual Care section in 1937. The cemeteries of Colma observed the thirties as every decade – with stories few stop to hear, though their portraits remain to tell.

With the bombing of Pearl Harbor in 1941, San Francisco became the launching pad to the Pacific islands. Donald Adanza (p. 79), 11, died that year. He was followed by Howard Lee (p. 40), 31, in 1942. This decade served as a turning point in America's cultural and economic history. Referred to as the "Bookend Decades," the period from 1920 to 1940 was bracketed by two world wars. It produced a time of emphatic conflict and cultural change for California and the San Francisco Bay Area.

The memorial portraits of Holy Cross and Colma Valley reflect those conflicts and capture that change. One observes these unpredictable times in human terms through the people of the portraits. Through their faces that history is preserved and their stories re-emerge.

Photo-Gallery V

The Domachin Angel
presides over the Slavonic section at sunset

Families: Generations Together Through Time
The DeBono Family

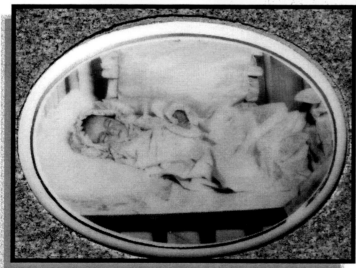

The DeBono Family

On August 11,1923 two-month old Frances DeBono died. Less than two weeks later her father, 52 year John (1871—1923), followed her. Wife and mother Claire DeBono (1883—1961) was buried with her family forty-three years later at age 78. The portrait of Frances is a postmortem photo showing her in her crib. Maria's portrait is a photograph re-traced with pen and ink to highlight faded sections.

The O'Brien Family

Anthony (1860–1899) and Julia O'Brien (died 1932) join their son, John P. O'Brien (1888–1923), and Julia's sister, Evelyn Story, in this Woodman sponsored grave. Woodman memorials began as a benefit from a fraternal organization founded in 1883. The society has now evolved into a several insurance companies. Original Woodmen members would pass a hat to guarantee the purchase of a headstone for the deceased. Anthony O'Brien's portrait is the oldest in Holy Cross and the oldest in Forgotten Faces. The monument, with its portraits, displays strong family tradition and continuity.

The Judnich Family Stone

Martin, Anna, Annie, Mary and Anton Judnich

Martin Judnich (1875—1947) and Anna Judnich (1875—1947) lost two daughters both at one year of age, Annie in 1905 and Mary in 1911. Their son Anton (1911—1939) was born two weeks after Mary died. He passed away at age 28. Martin and Anna died six months apart in 1947.

Mothers and Daughters

Elsie and Bertha Buehler
Elsie died in 1911 at the age of 8, her mother died six years later at the age of 38 in 1917. Elsie wears a lace dress and carries a ruffled parasol with a basketful of flowers for her studio portrait.

Nancy and Mary Garasemowicz,

Nancy (1887—1943) died at 56, losing her 11 year old daughter Mary (1911—1918) when Nancy was 31 years old. In her portrait, Mary appears to pout while wearing a faux sailor suit.

Fathers and Daughters

Andrew Lutich
1883—1917 Age 34

Camille lost her father when she was ten. She lived just 11 more years.

Camille Lutich
1907—1928 Age 21

Antoine and Florence Font

Father Antoine (1854 —1924) died at age 70, just six days before his daughter Florence (1897— 1924) at age 27.

Mothers and Their Sons Who Died Young

August and Maria Ghiberla

August (1888—1910)   Maria (1867—1921)

August died at age 22 when his mother was 43. The photo used for Maria's portrait has been retouched.
Her right hand originally rested on a child's shoulder or piece of furniture.

Rose and Paul Rauschan

Rose (1894—1927)   Paul (1912—1935)

Both died young: Rose at age 33, her son Paul eight years later at 23.
Rose is a native of Hungary.

Germaine and Gustove Grialou

Gustove (1909–1919)   *Germaine* (1876–1947)

Germaine lost her son when she was 43 and he was ten years old. He was born when she was 33. Gustove's photo was probably taken in his home where a vase and other furniture serve as the backdrop for his photo. Like a proud general in parade of his troops he holds a staff in faux salute, his left hand akimbo.

Fathers and Sons

Michel Lacu

Born in France, 1870, died in SF 1919 Age 49

Louis Lacu

1901 — 1924 Age 23

Mate Vukovich

1906 — 1921 Age 15
Mate's portrait is a photograph of a painting.

Ignacio Vukovich

1875 — 1934 Age 59
Ignacio is a native of Czechoslovakia.

Couples: The Eternal Bond of Matrimony

Louise's photo was taken around the turn of the century while Antonin's was made about 30 years later.

Louise and Antonin Garaudel

Louise (1871 — 1926)   *Both born in France*   *Antonin (1863 — 1940)*

Ermanno Parensi
1860 to March 25, 1933

Declinda Parensi
1860 to Oct. 12, 1933

The Parensi's portrait is a composite of two separate photos combined by the photographer to have the couple appear together.

Rudolpho and Palmira Mei

Rudolpho (1845—1914) Age 69, Palmira (1850—1913) Age 63 of Chivizzan, Italy.

◄ ***Scafani***
*In memory of my
beloved husband Luigi
1851—1921
(no other inscription)*

Duffy ►
Jeanette
(died July 4, 1923)
Edward
(died May 1, 1924)

Luciano Resquites
"Born Jaunuary 7, 1900, died December 30, 1926."
Native of Banga Capiz, Philipines.

Luciano's attention to detail is apparent in his carefully folded
handkerchief and perfectly positioned tie tack which coordinate well
with his three piece suit.

Mercedes DeLira Smith
Died June 9, 1918   Age 24 years, 8 months
Born in Mexico, Mercedes married J.A. Smith
and lived in Oakland, CA.

Gertrude Walker *died Feb. 25, 1922 at age 29*
Charles Walker *Feb. 18, 1922 to Feb. 22, 1922*
Their story hides between the lines of their epitaphs.

Mother and Son

Julia Rivolta
May 29, 1896 — May 12, 1919   Age 22

Julia's portrait is a photograph of a

Antonio X. Vieira
1878—1921   Age 43

Lena Spaich
1871—1923   Age 52

Native of Portugal

Native of Austria

Joseph Cozgaria *1862—1925 Age 63*
Joseph's stylized mustache is brushed upward.
Antonio and Joseph sport different style collars
with similar accessories.

James McNally
Died March 30, 1918 Age 48
James adds individuality to his formal
attire with a western style hat

**Guadelupe Madrid Vera
and Manuel Pegueros**

*Mexica-born Lupe is buried with
her "dear husband" Manuel.*

Guadelupe 1914 – 1937   Manuel 1890 – 1933

Angela V. Arraiz

May 5, 1899 — July 15, 1926   Age 27
Angela sports pearls with a curl.

Francis Bzik *1885 — 1930*

Born in Yugoslavia, Francis wears a flowered
garland and holds a bouquet. She died age 45.

Julienne and Ernest Cabot

Julienne and Ernest were both born in Decazeville, France 1877. Julienne died
in San Francisco in 1919 and Ernest also died in the city one year later.

The "Membership of the Moustache" bridges many nationalities.

Josef Anderholden

1859 — 1925   Age 66, Sweden

Jules Hoch

Died January 27, 1913   Age 49, Germany

Louis Broussal

Died in 1922   Age 49, France

Barny Guglielmietti

1868 — 1925   Age 57, Italy

Jose Bermudez

1903 — 1932   Age 29

Charlyne Witherby

1907 — 1924   Age 17

Margrete Talo O'Neill

Mary May Green

Dec. 12, 1904 — Sept. 22, 1925
*Her portrait reveals the occupation her
epitaph did not.*

Died October 12, 1925, age unknown
*Mary and Jose strike poses that
communicate much about them.*

John Franusich
Born in Dalmacia (Croatia) 1870, died in California 1926
John's high collar, hands thrust in his pockets and proud posture show him as a man of business.

Maria Lino
1862—1931 Age 69

Mary Cordtz
November 22, 1862 to February 16, 1923

Mary Matelycek
1872—1945
Age 73

John Sherry
1880—1937
Native of Malta   Age 57

Rose Morel

July 25, 1846 — May 31, 1925, Age 78

Rose wears an ornate metal collar clasp in early 20th-century style.

Rose's photograph represents portraiture in its most classic form. This studio portrait shows the subject in a head to shoulders view, her gaze at a 30 degree angle away from the camera and wearing formal attire with her hair pinned back. It documents Rose at her best so friends and family, in other places and other times, would observe, know and appreciate its her attributes.

The Somps Angel
stands sentinel
at the entrance to
Holy Cross Cemetery.

CHAPTER TEN

Rembrandts in the Attic: The Importance of Documenting Memorial Portraits

Like Rembrandts in the attic, memorial portraits represent lost treasures. Unlike Rembrandts, they are exposed to potential destruction. Every day, whether by the assault of nature or the hand of man, important remnants of our nation's past vanish.

Many simply fall off their headstones and remain intact. Although the ceramic portraits are made to last hundreds of years, the bonding materials in the early 1900s were not always durable. Portraits that separate from their gravestone can be picked up by any passer-by who might, unaware of their importance, discard or keep them. Some show up for sale on the Internet as "antiques" to be purchased by those uninformed or unconcerned about their origins. Whether separated from their mountings, damaged by weather or abruptly shattered by thoughtless vandalism, these relics are being lost much too rapidly. Industry experts confirm that in most cemeteries there are as many damaged, destroyed and missing portraits as those remaining intact.

More people steal or destroy these relics than photograph them. More people steal or destroy these relics than photograph them. These valued works of art justify more concern. Their individual and collective insights merit preservation.

The Mission of *Forgotten Faces*

As a key component of our mission statement (p. 191), *Forgotten Faces* hopes to raise this issue and alert readers to this problem. We encourage genealogists, historians, cemetery enthusiasts and interested parties to contact cemetery management and obtain permission to systematically survey their local cemeteries and photograph memorial portraits from this era. Provide cemetery officials with a copy of the results for their records. Most will be receptive to the idea. Show them a copy of *Forgotten Faces* and convey the importance of this art as an asset – to the cemetery, to the nation and to our collective history. Few understand the importance these relics represent beyond the borders of their own memorial parks.

Once destroyed, the portraits cannot be retrieved. Once photographed, their images are captured and preserved forever. They can then be distributed to family members or others and preserved for the valued history they represent. If appropriate, they can even be duplicated and restored to their original state or replace the original if it is damaged or missing. Our goal is to reverse the current trend and have more people photographing and documenting these works of art than destroying them.

Locating Memorial Portraits from the Early 20th Century

To preserve memorial portraits you have to know where they are. Several variables increase the likelihood of finding porcelain memorial portraits from the early 20th century. Cemetery rules and regulations, the age of the cemetery, the ethnic mix of those interred in the cemetery and the proximity of portrait suppliers all influence the probability of finding portraits.

Some cemeteries prohibit memorial portraits. As Lisa Montanarelli noted in Chapter Two, Catholic cemeteries in Philadelphia, for example, made this official policy in 1942. However, many cemeteries in the area still possess portraits mounted prior to this time.

The age of the cemetery often determines the likelihood of finding portraits from this era. Locate cemeteries that were accepting interments from around 1900 to 1920. In some circumstances, newer burial grounds may have accepted interments from older city cemeteries forced to re-inter in suburban locations. These prescribed areas will often be marked or defined either by signage or descriptions in cemetery literature. The cemetery administrator can direct you to the oldest sections of the cemetery.

The two simplest, most effective means of finding information on cemeteries in your area is the phone book and the Internet. Local Yellow Pages list cemeteries and sometimes provide descriptions including their founding date. Call and ask if they have or allow memorial portraits. Many larger cities still have smaller cemeteries within their city limits so do not overlook them.

Local road maps mark cemeteries in distinct shades and coloring. Not all cemeteries, especially the smaller ones, are included on modern road maps but the larger and older ones usually are. Rand McNally maps are particularly good at designating cemeteries. Laurel Gabel, an experienced AGS member and lecturer adds, "U.S. Geodetic Survey Maps mark all known cemeteries with a distinctive symbol and are a fairly reliable cemetery finding tool."

Many cemeteries located in rural areas contain a few memorial portraits from the early 1900s. Some even contain rare and unusual portraits. Major cemeteries in Sacramento, the capital of California, contain very few memorial portraits; however, smaller cemeteries nearer the Sierra foothills typically have five to 10 ceramic portraits from this era. Memorial portraits from the early 20th century can turn up anywhere immigrants settled.

Internet Resources for Locating Cemeteries

The Internet is quick and helpful for finding listings of cemeteries. Type in the name of the town where you are looking followed by the word "cemeteries" into your search engine of choice and you will typically receive listings of cemeteries there and nearby. Add the word "links," as in "*Cityname* cemetery links," and this search will generate links to many cemeteries and cemetery organizations locally, nationally and internationally.

Four excellent online sources for locating and understanding cemetery etiquette and lore are Cemetery Junction (http://www.cemeteryjunction.com/), Interment.Net (www.Interment.net), the Association for Gravestone Studies (www.GraveStoneStudies.ORG) and the Tombstone Transcription Project (www.rootsweb.com/~cemetery).

Cemetery Junction, Interment.net and the Tombstone Transcription Project are free, comprehensive and provide links with many additional resources and useful information. Cemetery Junction provides information and links to every major cemetery in the nation. Interment.net provides a similarly comprehensive set of online resources.

AGS, the Association of Gravestone Studies, is a wealth of excellent information, resources and expertise on cemeteries and gravestones. Founded in 1977, AGS has a superb library and store, sponsors subject-specific conferences and seminars, offers scholarships for selected studies, and provides some of the most enthusiastic and informed individuals in the industry as resources. Annual membership dues start at $20 for students and $50 for individuals. AGS is one of the most comprehensive and well-schooled organizations on the study of cemeteries and gravestones in the nation.

The Tombstone Transcription Project is an ambitious national effort with local representatives in most states. Through volunteers the project seeks to document and preserve epitaphs and gravestone inscriptions at cemeteries across the nation. It maintains a large database that fulfills the goals of this ample project.

If you are in the South, check out *The Tombstone Traveler's Guide* at www.tombstonetravel.com/index.html. Designed and maintained by ChrisTina Leimer, it contains a wealth of information on cemeteries in Southern states. Leimer provides valuable information on cemetery etiquette, tradition and many links to other cemeteries, national and international, including numerous photographs.

All of these resources can help you to understand the issues cemetery directors face and how you can best work with them to make your project and their jobs easier.

Rules and Regulations: Working with Cemetery Directors/Managers

Cemetery administrators and workers have tough duty. They interact with families during times of grief and confusion. People, rightfully, feel very possessive about their family's gravestones. They want them protected. They adamantly defend any representation of the family member they lost. But in these fiscally conservative times, cemetery maintenance budgets are squeezed, endowment funds limited and pressures to cut costs constant. The deceased cannot defend themselves. Cemetery regulations often seem unnecessarily rigid, impersonal and unfriendly. "No Flowers Allowed." "No Christmas Decorations Allowed." "Cemetery Closed at 3 p.m." Administrators enforce policy, they don't write it. If you are communicative and understanding with cemetery officials you will find they try their best to respond accordingly. They are often caught, literally, between a stone and an inflexible rule.

Permission to Publish Your Photographs

Although most cemeteries allow daytime access to graves and mausoleums, some do not allow pictures to be taken without the family's permission. Although cemeteries must allow public access for the visitation of graves, most cemeteries are private property. If they allow photographs, publishing family information (specifically names) on gravestone for public distribution normally requires cemetery permission. Taking pictures for personal use is usually allowed unless otherwise posted. But if you plan to publish pictures of headstones displaying family names, permission from the cemetery is required to avoid legal complications. Pictures that do not display specific family surnames are less problematic. Photographs without any identifying names, including the cemetery of origin, generate even less concern. Such unidentified photographs used as instructive examples and free of inflammatory commentary are normally acceptable. In European countries, with older, more celebrated cemeteries, photography may be less restrictive in this regard.[13] However, obtaining permission removes all doubt and is always the best course of action if you expect to publish your photographs.

Locating Memorial Portraits from the Early 20th Century

Where are you most likely to find memorial portraits from the early 20th century? As noted, the art was popularized by the Italians and its use spread across

Southern and Eastern Europe. These populations brought the tradition with them to the United States.

European nations where such portraits often can be found include England, Ireland, Italy, France, Portugal and Spain. Eastern European countries include Austria, Poland, Lithuania, Russia, Serbia, Croatia, Ukraine, Romania, Czechoslovakia and Yugoslavia. Immigrants from these countries provide opportunities for finding memorial portraits from the early 1900s.

Older Catholic and Jewish cemeteries often harbor large concentrations of this funerary art. Nondenominational cemeteries normally provide fewer opportunities to locate portraits but sometimes have sections dedicated to specific nationalities that do. Catholic and Jewish cemeteries with nationalities from Southern and Eastern European ancestry, particularly Italian Catholic, offer the most opportunity for locating turn-of-the-century memorial portraits. Traditionally, Mexico and the South American countries Brazil, Chile and Peru have also included portraits on gravestones. Immigrants from there during this period are a valued source of portraits. I am told the home countries yield notable numbers of memorial portraits.

Cleaning Memorial Portraits

If you find a beautiful old portrait covered with lichen and stained from grass clippings, you can clean the porcelain. The ONLY cleaning paraphernalia appropriate to use on memorial portraits is a soft cloth soaked in water. Do NOT use cleaners or solvents of any type. The turn-of-the-century resins used to encase portraits were not made with modern solvents and chemical cleaning agents in mind. Using acetone or

Vandalized Portraits

These two portraits are typical of vandalized portraits that remain on the headstone. The one on the far left was shot with a BB or pellet gun, the other deliberately scored with a chisel or other sharp object.

---

[13] http://www.photo.net/bboard

alcohol-based products such as glass or shower cleaners may permanently cloud the transparent resin. Use only a soft cloth and water, or you might transform a dirty portrait into a permanently damaged one.

Portraits in Need of Repair

How do you repair a damaged memorial portrait? Unless it is your family, you don't. Do not attempt to repair or remount a memorial portrait yourself. It requires expertise you likely do not have.

If you happen upon a portrait that is broken, cracked, faded or separated from its headstone, write the name, epitaph and location of the stone and bring it and the separated portrait to the cemetery administration. However, unless the grave is of a direct relative, don't expect much. Except for remounting intact portraits, cemeteries do not repair memorial portraits. If the headstone belongs to your family, you can have the portrait taken to a monument maker to attempt repair. Expertise in doing so varies from none to some. Often a damaged portrait is damaged forever.

The more likely approach is to locate another photograph of the subject and have a new portrait made. If you find a portrait that has fallen from its stone, document it by name and location (note the names of the stones on the left and right as well), and bring the portrait and notations to cemetery management. Do not try to reapply any portrait to a headstone even if it belongs to your family. The task is best done by cemetery professionals. Experts sand the surface of the stone and use powerful adhesives that keep out moisture and last indefinitely. You especially don't want to cement the wrong portrait to an incorrect headstone. (It's been done!)

Methods for Photographing Memorial Portraits

The most important service you can provide for the preservation of a memorial portrait is to permanently capture its image and headstone information with high-resolution photographs. The following is a proven method for doing so.

Start by photographing the entire headstone, including the name and epitaph. Avoid patterns of mixed sun and shade. If possible, use an umbrella or coat to shield the gravestone from direct sunlight, which often generates too much contrast and creates harsh shadows that obscure detail.

Next, take a picture of the headstone from 10-12 feet away and include one or two surrounding headstones. This helps to relocate the stone as well as illustrate its setting. Next take close-ups of the epitaph and other inscriptions to record them in detail. Follow the same sequence of photographs with each stone – overview of whole stone, surrounding location, epitaph and then the portrait close up. Keeping to this pattern (or one of your choice) will help you locate and database your photographs more easily when you get home. Now you are ready to document the photograph itself.

When you photograph the selected portrait, shoot it at least twice, each time checking your focus and exposure. Bracket exposures if you like; many digital cameras have settings to do that automatically.

Use either of two methods for a close-up of the portrait that fills the entire viewfinder of your camera without cutting off any edges of the portrait's oval outline. You may want to turn the camera sideways, using portrait mode to properly match the height of its oval shape. This puts more of the portrait in the picture, allowing more detail for close-ups or enlargements.

If your camera has a macro feature you may want to use it. Macro allows you to take photographs in great detail from very close range – a matter of inches. The difficulty with macro photography is that it requires a lot of light and a tripod to reduce blurring induced by minor movements and low light. Do not use a flash to add light because its brightness will wash out your picture or parts of it and make it useless. If you choose to use the macro feature of your camera, bring a tripod so you can hold steady without blurring due to minor movement. You may also want to bring a reflective umbrella or white jacket to deflect natural light onto the stone, offsetting shadows or fending off harsh sunlight.

A simpler way to capture a close-up without a macro lens utilizes the zoom function of your camera. Most modern cameras possess this feature. Standing several feet from the portrait, zoom in on it until the portrait fills your viewfinder. This approach allows more natural light on the subject and frees you from using a tripod under most circumstances. Light permitting, you can also decrease your shutter speed to less than $1/500^{th}$ of a second to stop blurring cause by movement. (Professional photographers *always* prefer a tripod to get razor-sharp focus.) If you are documenting the portraits for personal or family use, this approach will normally produce perfectly acceptable photos. However, if your objective is to produce high-resolution photographs capable of 8"x10" reproductions or larger, a tripod is always preferable. Unavoidable hand movement reduces the sharpness of the photograph while a tripod assures a rock-solid shot capable of quality enlargement and reproduction.

If you use a film camera, try a 400 ASA film rating to provide proper exposure in shade. If you find a particularly beautiful portrait or plan on very large reproductions, you may want to use a large-format camera that produces a 4"x6" or larger negative. Also, read John Yang's technical notes in the appendix of his book, *Mount Zion Sepulchral Portraits,* for useful hints and guidelines regarding this technology and its professional application to memorial portraits.

If you use a digital camera, take the photograph in the highest resolution possible – a fine or superfine jpeg or TIFF file. Use raw files if you prefer them.

When taking the picture, try to avoid shadows (especially your own) that cover portions of the portrait or headstone. Avoid reflections from the sun on the portrait's shiny ceramic surface. Photographs of porcelain portraits taken in open shade with ambient light generally produce better quality reproductions than those taken in direct sunlight. The results are more uniform in color and shading.

Little can be done to salvage portraits whose picture has faded from exposure to the sun and weather. That is why taking a photograph of it, which will not age or change, is the most appropriate and positive thing you can do to preserve the image.

How to Make a Booklet of Portrait Photographs

Do you want to make a simple, inexpensive but attractive black-and-white booklet out of your photographs? Here is a quick and easy set of PC tools and software that produces quality booklets in minutes.

Obtain the software programs *FinePrint* (www.Fineprint.com) or *Clickbook* (www.BlueSquirrel.com/clickbook), which automatically generate booklet formats from standard word-processing applications. These established products cost less than $50 and print any word-processing documents in 5x8" booklet format on standard 8½"x11" paper. They are fast, simple to use and produce quality results.

Select the photographs and place them in your favorite word-processing software with the design and page layout you prefer. One picture per page displays the photos well and is simple to lay out. Add more pictures on a page if you like. Portrait length, which matches the natural oval shape of portraits, works best.

After installing the booklet-making software it functions like any printer. You simply "print" the file to the selected software in your file/print menu and it formats your word-processing doc into a booklet design. Submit the resulting file to your hard-copy printer and you will produce a presentable 5"x8" booklet. You also need a long-reach saddle stapler to staple the folded pages to properly bind the booklet.

Or you can print your document in 81/2"x11" format and staple the left side. Use any of the numerous presentation bindings to display your book. If you took your photos with film or with a quality, 5 mega-pixel and up digital camera, they will reproduce well at this size, retaining their original detail and sharpness.

If you wish to make more than 10 copies of your booklet you may want take your document to a quality reproduction or copy center. Many offer booklet reformatting as a standard option so you can bring them 81/2"x11" files, which they reproduce in 5"x8" format. To do this you will need to convert your word-processing document to an industry standard PDF – Portable Document Format. Using a PDF assures that the colors and formatting you see in your document are accurately reproduced by the printer. If you use your standard word-processing software, be prepared for annoying color and formatting surprises. It is best to use PDFs to assure proper reproduction. Kinko's offers its own PDF conversion software called KDF. It is a free download from their Website but only works for Kinko stores. It performs well and saves the cost of purchasing PDF software.

To obtain a PDF-producing software, try *Adobe Acrobat,* which is not exactly inexpensive at $300 but is the industry standard. However, *PDF Producer, Jaws PDF Creator, FinePrint PDF Factory,* among others, are all available for less than $60 and produce high-quality PDF documents that meet all printing standards. In addition to *Adobe Acrobat*, I recommend *Jaws PDF Creator* because it reproduces graphic-intensive content well.

These software products work similarly to the booklet software. You select them as a "print" option and choose the quality of the reproduction you want. Remember, the better the quality the larger the file. Use 300 or 600 dpi resolution and copy the resultant file to a CD. Bring the CD to your printer and ask for 5"x8" booklet format on 28-lb. laser quality paper and you'll be the proud owner of a memorial portrait collection. You can design and make your own cover. Follow the same process and have the cover produced on glossy 80-lb. or heavier stock. The printer will collate, fold and staple the booklet for you. The result is rewarding and presentable at an affordable price.

How to Build a Quick and Easy Website for Your Memorial Portraits

Want your own Website to display your memorial portrait collection? You can have your own Website up in an hour and running for less than $60 per year.

Register a domain name at www.register.com , www.domaindirect.com or the domain registry of your choice. Choose and register your unique domain name and select the free or bundled Website package all these vendors offer. The site is either free with the registration (Register.com offers *Website Now* at no cost) or comes bundled with the value of the registration package you choose (DomainDirect provides a *Web Identity* bundled site). Either of these vendors allows you to start building your Website immediately after you register your unique domain name. The site construction is menu-driven and allows a variety of design options. These low-cost sites do not offer online purchasing capabilities. That will cost you more and requires access to Website code available with more expensive options.

If you'd rather display than sell your collection, most of these low-cost sites offer three pages of photos. You can also receive e-mails from site visitors and provide links to other Websites. These options offer excellent value for their price. The sites look attractive and function like any Website, though they often contain some sponsor advertising.

This process allows you to have a functioning Website in an hour – if you have all your photos selected and ready to download at 72 dpi resolution – at an affordable price.

Preserving Our Legacy: The Value of Photographing Memorial Portraits

Photographing memorial portraits assures them a future to accompany their esteemed past. Recording portraits by photographic reproduction remains the simplest and most useful action anyone can take to preserve these images.

How valuable would it be now if someone had photographed the scores of children's postmortem portraits reported in Chicago before they were stolen? It would even be possible to use those photographs now to replace the originals. Memorial portraits are always limited to their location in a physical cemetery. Quality photographic documentation has no geographic boundaries and lasts indefinitely. It may also be easily reproduced and circulated to relatives, archivists and museums. If desired, digital photographs can be restored and the original image refurbished with photo-editing software to appear virtually new. This is accomplished while the integrity of the original photo remains uncompromised.

Documentation provides the best of both worlds. The original photograph remains a valuable record with its inherent historical value intact. A restored photograph can represent the portrait at its best before decay or degeneration set in.

Capturing the image of the portrait with a high-resolution photograph preserves our individual and collective heritage. It offers new life for family members who desire to honor and perpetuate the image of their loved one. The original photographer would understand and approve. It acknowledges and perpetuates their work. Future enthusiasts may again appreciate their efforts. Photographic preservation provides many benefits without any significant disadvantages.

Forgotten Faces began as a singular attempt to capture old images that were simply too beautiful to pass by. Now you are viewing them in print, renewed with life and presence. Thousands more await discovery and preservation. If not, their fate may be to turn into an empty oval space on a tombstone without a face.

Forgotten Faces represents a call to action. It urges all knowledgeable and interested parties to initiate this conservation process and begin documenting memorial portraits in their regions. With their efforts, all our urban and rural cemeteries will soon produce thousands of beautiful and rarely seen treasures from our immigrant past. I, for one, can hardly wait. Document and preserve these national treasures now. Behind their eyes peering back at us from decades past, you may sense the satisfaction evident in that lasting smile.

Resources and Related Reading

This list is meant to compliment the material in *Forgotten Faces* and is not a comprehensive listing of all available industry organizations or reading material.

Organizations:

❖ **The Association for Gravestone Studies**
278 Main Street, Suite 207
Greenfield, Massachusetts 01301
www.GravestoneStudies.org

❖ **Tombstone Transcription Project** - www.rootsweb.com/~cemetery/
Transcribes tombstone inscriptions into a common database.

❖ **California Historical Society** - www.californiahistoricalsociety.org/
A wealth of information on California history.

❖ **Society of Dutch Enamellers:** Information on Photo-Ceramic Enamels on glass and metal
www.enamellers.nl/english/carpenter1.htm
A detailed description of the history and process of enamels on ceramics.

Related Reading and Viewing:

❖ *Mount Zion: Sepulchral Portraits*   Distributed Arts Publishers, New York NY
by John Yang   Available at www.Amazon.com; and Barnes and Noble stores/on-line

❖ *The Collector's Guide to Early Photographs* 1st and 2nd Editions Krause Publications, Iola WI
By O. Henry Mace   Available at www.Amazon.com; and Barnes and Noble stores/on-line

❖ *Uncovering Your Ancestry through Family Photographs*   Betterway Books, Cincinnati OH
By Maureen Taylor   Available at www.Amazon.com; and Barnes and Noble stores/on-line

❖ *Your Guide to Cemetery Research*   Betterway Books, Cincinnati OH
By Sharon DeBartolo Carmack   Available at www.Amazon.com; Barnes and Noble stores/on-line

❖ *Secure the Shadow: Death and Photography in America*   Massachusetts Institute of Technology
By Jay Ruby   Available at www.Amazon.com; and Barnes and Noble stores/on-line

❖ *Dressed for the Photographer: Ordinary Americans and Fashion* 1840-1900 Kent State U. Press, OH
By Joan Severa   Available at www.Amazon.com; and Barnes and Noble stores/on-line

❖ *Unlocking the Secrets in Old Photographs*   Ancestry Salt Lake City, UY
By Karen Frisch-Ripley   Available at www.Amazon.com; and Barnes and Noble stores/on-line

❖ DVD – *Death in America* - a video documentary on death and it's effects on American Society
By Dr. Stanley Burns, produced by J.R. Olivero Available at 800-322-6502 **or** www.DeathinAmerica.com

❖ *Legal Handbook for Photographers: the Rights and Liabilities of Making Images* Amherst Media
By Bert p. Krages   Available at www.Amazon.com; and Barnes and Noble stores/on-line

❖ *Graveyards of Chicago: The People, History, Art and Lore of Cook County Cemeteries*
By Matt Hucke and Ursula Bielski   Available at www.Amazon.com; Barnes and Noble stores/on-line
Lake Claremont Press, Chicago

❖ *Stories in Stone: A Field Guide to Cemetery Symbolism and Iconography*   Henry Holt and Company
By Doug Keister   Available at www.Amazon.com; Barnes and Noble stores/on-line

Resources and related reading: Continued

US Manufacturers of Memorial Portraits:

❖ **Paradise Pictures** – a source for quality memorial portraits with comprehensive guarantees. 2901 Neal Road, Paradise, CA 95967-3190   Toll Free - 800.960.8040 http://www.paradisepictures.com/index.htm, email: info@paradisepictures.com

❖ **Permaframe Inc**. – another source for memorial portraits with comprehensive guarantees. 7040 W. Palmetto Park, Road., #4-613 Boca Raton, FL 33433, Toll free - (800) 55-PERMA (73762) e-mail: Permaframe@adelphia.net, www.permaframe.com/

❖ **J A Dedouch Co** – U.S. manufacturer of memorial portraits for the last century. 608 Harrison St., Oak Park, IL 60304   Phone: 708-386-1130, Fax: 708-386-2671

❖ **Oak Park Ceramic Company** – 15 Hillside Ave., Hillside, IL 60162 (tel. 708-449-5158).

European Sources of Memorial Portraits:

❖ **Italian Memorial Products, Rossato Giovanni** – 1 – P.O. Box 524 – 36100 Vicenza, Italy Phone – (39) 0444-928499 – Fax (39) 04440928711 – email: info@italian-memorial-products.com

❖ **Photokeramik,** Josef Günthner GmbH, Melicharstrasse 4a, 4020 Linz, Austria (tel. +43 (0) 732 65 14 88, fax. +43 (0) 732 65 14 88 4, or by e-mail: josef.guenthner@photokeramik.at)

❖ **Willems Classics**, Joost v.d. Vondellaan 37, 1422 HK Uithoorn, the Netherlands (tel. +31-(0)297-524040, fax +31-(0)297-524042, e-mail emaille@willemsclassics.nl

❖ **Italian Memorial Products, Rossato Giovanni** – 1 – P.O. Box 524 – 36100 Vicenza, Italy Phone – (39) 0444-928499 – Fax (39) 04440928711 – email: info@italian-memorial-products.com

Useful InterNet Links for finding Cemeteries and related interests:

❖ **Cindy's List** – the most exhaustive on-line listings of genealogy and ancestry information available at no charge. **http://www.cyndislist.com/**

❖ **Free Genealogy Service** provides comprehensive listings to all the major genealogy services and resources - www.heaven4me.com/geneology.html

❖ **Society Hill Directory** provides useful information and a wealth of on-line links to historical societies all across the United States   www.daddezio.com/society/index.html

❖ **Cemetery Junction** serves as the center point for finding any cemetery in the United States that has on line services as well as valuable information about cemeteries.   www.cemeteryjunction.com/

❖ **Interment.Net** is an on-line service that allows you to browse cemetery transcriptions collected all over the United States   www.Interment.net

INDEX

Forgotten Faces – Our Mission Statement

Forgotten Faces is a book with a mission. Below, I define objectives that I hope this book attained. Please contact me at www.ForgottenFaces.org if you feel I have not adequately accomplished the stated goals or have additional suggestions for its improvement. I genuinely appreciate your interest and feedback.

Forgotten Faces acknowledges the contribution of memorial portraits to art and history. We endeavor to:

1) celebrate memorial portraiture as a distinctive art form. Developed by European artisans in the 19th century, their oval shapes, sepia tones and period fashions embody artistry encapsulated in time.

2) treat the portraits as historical artifacts. Alone, a portrait functions as a time capsule from another era. Collectively, the portraits provide insights into our ancestral and cultural heritage.

3) present a large selection of portraits in excellent condition, despite almost a century of climatic wear.

4) demonstrate the ethnic diversity of early 20th century Californians.

5) explore the technology that combined precious metals with photographs to create an image capable of sustaining the intense heat of a kiln and survive the elements for almost a century.

6) appreciate how these photographs bring life to the cemeteries and connect us to the departed by "providing encounters with the living in the very land of the dead."

7) alert readers to the fact that more of these artifacts are destroyed each day and recommend methods for documenting them. We encourage others to record these valued relics from our past.

8) open a window in time on the faces of California and America's immigrant past. Forgotten by the lens of history their portraits reveal their stories through the light of the photographer's eye.

[1] Gary Collison Editor of *Markers*, the journal of the Association of Gravestone Studies

Ronald William Horne 2004

Field Notes